OPPORTUNITY KNOCKS

OPPORTUNITY KNOCKS

HOW HARD WORK, COMMUNITY, AND BUSINESS CAN IMPROVE LIVES AND END POVERTY

SENATOR
TIM SCOTT

CENTER
STREET®

NASHVILLE   NEW YORK

Center Street
Hachette Book Group
1290 Avenue of the Americas, New York, NY 10104
centerstreet.com
twitter.com/centerstreet

First Edition: April 2020

Center Street is a division of Hachette Book Group, Inc. The Center Street
name and logo are trademarks of Hachette Book Group, Inc.

The publisher is not responsible for websites (or their content)
that are not owned by the publisher.

Print book interior design by Timothy Shaner, NightandDaydesign.biz.

Library of Congress Control Number: 2020932494

ISBNs: 978-1-5460-5913-4 (hardcover), 978-1-5460-5912-7 (ebook)

Printed in the United States of America

LSC-C

10 9 8 7 6 5 4 3 2 1

This book is dedicated to my grandparents Artis and Louida Ware. When I was in the greatest need with nothing to offer, they took me in and loved me with the riches in their hearts while sharing their limited resources abundantly.

To my mother, my living hero! Thank you for your prayers, your encouragement, patience, and the constant love you gave me every single day. Without you, I don't exist! May God continue to bless you with "exceedingly, abundantly above all you can ask or imagine." Ephesians 3:20-21

CONTENTS

OPPORTUNITY KNOCKS

White House Photo / Shealah Craighead

CHAPTER 1

AN AMERICAN
PASSAGE

ON A MUGGY, overcast September day in 2017, I stood in the cool, quiet bustle of the White House, just outside the Oval Office, waiting to see the president of the United States. In the wake of my negative critique of his comments on the race riot inspired by neo-Nazis in Charlottesville a few weeks earlier, Donald Trump had sent word that we needed to talk.

In comments enthusiastically reported by the media, I had said that the president's statements compromised his moral authority and his reaction showed an insensitivity on racial issues. As the only black Republican United States senator, my comments had clearly struck a hot nerve with my Republican president.

With me that day was Jennifer DeCasper, my chief of staff, who had accompanied me on the ride over from the Capitol. The ride was short in distance but long in nervous anticipation of what we might face when we arrived. Jennifer had walked with me along some of our thornier paths throughout my time in Congress. Her faith and sharp wit seemed to make those walks easier.

And now, there in the car, I told Jennifer that we needed to pray, to ask the Lord for clarity and guidance in this unusual and possibly contentious meeting. She agreed that we needed to keep the Lord in the middle of all we were doing and then added: "Can you also ask that when this is over, I am still fully employable? I have a kid, you know." I had to smile, for I knew in my heart He would be with us all the way.

To be sure, President Trump's displeasure over my comments had a political sting for me as well as for him. Trump was very popular in South Carolina, and plenty of my constituents were displeased with me and claimed that I had been unfair to Trump. So, it was important to me that I do my best to help the president understand why I strongly disagreed with his assessment and to look for some common ground. I hoped that beneath his public bluster, the president felt the same way as I.

In weighing this dicey situation, I kept in mind that there are some things more important than politics—namely, that while there may be an ebb and flow in politics, I am going to be black for the rest of my life. I have never doubted that the good Lord had a purpose in making me black—and maybe it was for just such a time as this. For all of my life and for all of my family's heritage, we had tried to avoid being confrontational. Always, we believed, the primary aim should be to find common ground in order to move forward.

As we made our way through the multiple layers of security checkpoints, I caught the eyes of almost everyone I interacted with. As they returned the glance, I wondered if they knew why I was there. Were the black faces looking back at me applauding me? Hoping I would stand up for their invisible pain? Wondering if I would succeed? Did the white faces understand why I had to be there? Did they understand why this was important not only to me but to all people of color, as well as to the spirit of our country?

As we waited there in the White House for a few minutes, it all crystalized for me—the truth of who I am and how my direct ancestors survived the cruel Atlantic crossing from West Africa in the stinking, sweltering belly of slave ships, reaching American soil in the early 1800s. My family's DNA places our origins in Nigeria or Cameroon. At the end of their terrible passage, it seems clear that my direct forebears set foot on American soil at Charleston. There, they were sold at auction into human bondage to spend the rest of their days like beasts of burden, picking cotton in the broiling summer sun of South Carolina.

Now, I ask you to pause for a moment and consider what must have been the abject hopelessness of these people . . . their utter despair as they were disbursed across a strange new world known as the American Southland.

But somehow, *somehow*—and this is the divine hand of the Lord—as they settled into their new lives, some of them began to sense the tiniest flicker of hope in their hearts that right beyond their wretched present, things just might get a little bit better. It is impossible that any one of my ancestors envisioned a grand pageant in which the son of a son of a son of a slave would become a United States senator. More likely, the small hope was something more important to the moment like, maybe, *just maybe*, their master would give them an extra ration of meat for their Sunday meal. If my enslaved forebears had not been sustained by hope and faith, no matter how simple, then there would be no reason to keep picking cotton, even to the end of the row.

Just how my family got from then to now is an elusive journey that will never be known with any precision. Equally important is the fact that I will never understand the horrors of that journey. No matter how many prejudiced people I suffer, no matter how many offensive innuendos I encounter, I will never adequately appreciate what they endured. Whatever the details, I revere my ancestors for their courageous endurance and their faith that things might be better. I'm reminded of some advice I once got from Congressman John Lewis of Georgia, the legendary civil rights leader. He repeated some advice he had first shared with me in his office in 2011. This time, we were in Selma, Alabama, at the Edmund Pettus Bridge. He was describing what happened on Bloody Sunday in March 1965. John Lewis described the snarling dogs and the fire hoses and how he was terribly beaten by the police and left unconscious on the pavement.

It was heart-wrenching to hear the vivid, graphic observations from this courageous man who is my senior by a quarter century. And then he delivered some advice I've tried to live by. "Never, ever become bitter," he said. This is wonderful advice that I have followed since my youth because of my faith.

While I know and cherish the facts and forces that have made my success possible, I am also committed to never abandon my past. Indeed, that past is me and part of the steady continuum that is my present and future. I am committed to showing others how they, too, can come to taste and enjoy the fruits of the faith and principles that have girded who I am and how I got here.

Still, as a descendant of those in bondage, I found it emotionally reassuring to be waiting to meet with the most powerful person in the world—and to meet him on terms evened up by the full bloom of our nation's Constitution. This along with the hard political fact that I am the duly elected representative of more than five million American citizens in the State of South Carolina. No matter what happened in this meeting, I could not stand down from my belief that Trump's actual comments had shown a real insensitivity to the racial history of our country.

But I knew I had to keep these swirling emotions at bay. One of the strong lessons of my grandfather, about whom you will read much in this book, is to never let your emotions lead your words. You have to be dispassionate if you want others to listen. You must purge the emotional toxicity out of the equation. My job was to speak with the authority that the good Lord had given me to have this conversation with the most powerful person in the world—on his turf and in the Oval Office. These thoughts provided clarity and focus so that I could say what I thought was important. As was my habit, I chose my favorite pair of colorful socks in the great tradition of George H. W. Bush.

So, that is where we were as Jennifer and I were ushered into the Oval Office and greeted by a gracious and charming Donald Trump.

I had interacted with him in a positive way in the past. Whatever else, the man is authentic in his skin. If you don't like him, you probably never will. Who he is, he will always be. Once you know that, you can work with it. Prior to our meeting, I had seen him in a variety of circumstances and knew that he is a classic counterpuncher. If you hit him, he is going to hit back and keep punching until he's had enough and thinks he's won. That's just who he is.

In the Oval Office, we were sitting across from his desk and in front of the fireplace. In the pictures I saw later, my colorful-socks are shining brightly, but President Trump is dead serious, totally engaged and listening.

He asked me to explain my comments and to help him understand where he was off base. I went through what it is like to endure racism of any sort and how it affects all people of color. I told him how his comments that there were good people on both sides in the Charlottesville tragedy hurt my heart. I explained that my growing up decades ago in a much different South Carolina meant daily encounters that left me with an absolute sense of dejection, the sense of not being complete because of the color of my skin, and having it be reinforced on a daily basis. I explained how it leaves a stain that you can't get off, especially since you have done nothing wrong.

The president sat there quietly. Other than a few questions, a few flicks of his eyebrows, he really offered nothing beyond exuding an air of listening and understanding. I had expected hard, defensive pushback from him, but what I got back at the end was like sweet music from the angels, manna from heaven.

With a tone that I interpreted as sincere humility, he looked at me and quietly said, "Tell me what I can do to be helpful to the people I've offended."

I was authentically surprised. The president was offering an olive branch, and in what seemed like divine intervention, the good Lord had prepared me with the right answer for an important moment.

For decades, the federal government has struggled over how to tackle poverty. It was not for lack of effort or due to bad intentions, but rather from relying upon a faulty model. For more than fifty years, starting with President Lyndon Johnson's "Great Society," the federal government has dumped huge amounts of money into an ever-growing web of bureaucracy and red tape. Yet poverty rates remain basically unchanged since the early 1970s, especially in the black community. The safety net should be a trampoline catapulting folks toward success—not a trap that keeps people exactly where they are.

Perhaps it comes down to how we see human nature. I certainly know we all have our faults, and you'll read about some of mine later. But I also believe most people are good. It takes a pessimistic view of our fellow man and his potential to think he needs the government to take care of every single thing. That's why I believe that we have to change not only the way government is involved in helping those in need, but how we as a individuals help them as well.

In Luke, the Bible reminds us that to whom much is given, much is required. While it often seems that some want a culture war, pitting economic and racial classes against each other, I am looking to ignite a cultural renaissance. Some use envy or distrust as their engine; I want to use hope and opportunity to power a future where we work together to build a stronger country.

With those concepts in mind, my team and I, along with EIG, the Economic Innovation Group, had been working for several years on a concept called Opportunity Zones, a piece of legislation designed to give American businesses and individuals a way to invest freely in our nation's most distressed communities without the federal government getting in the way. Under this program, investors are given tax breaks for investing in areas designated as "opportunity zones," which are places that investors might not feel compelled to invest in without the tax incentives. For example, instead of building its new factory in a community that's already well-off and developed, a manufacturer might decide to put down roots in, say, a small tract of land outside Charleston, South Carolina, that's more in need of the economic boost.

The idea, of course, is to have these investors put down roots and become part of the communities they invest in. No flipping a burned-out rowhouse into a storage business and then leaving town. No putting up a five-star hotel in the middle of an empty street and then heading out as soon as the tax rebate kicks in. To qualify for the tax incentives, investors have to be serious about

their investments, getting to know the communities they're joining, ensuring that the people already living there are involved in
the decision making. In fact, investors can't even take advantage
of the tax breaks unless they keep their investments for at least
five years, and additional benefits don't kick in until they've been
in their communities for seven years.

If I've learned anything from studying our country's efforts to
combat poverty in the twentieth century, it's that business owners
know better than the government how to spend their money, and
I designed opportunity zones with that in mind. This was something I hoped President Trump, who'd been a developer and a
businessman all his life, would understand.

So, with a deep breath, I explained to President Trump my
belief that we must find fresh ways to alleviate the terrible poverty
that is the source of so many of our ills—including the plague of
racism. The concept of Opportunity Zones includes employing
incentives in the tax code to harness private money for investments into distressed communities.

President Trump was not aware that this idea was being
discussed in the Senate as we worked to put together the Tax Cut
and Jobs Act. I explained the highlights and concepts, adding that
what was most needed, at the very moment we were talking, was
a big push from the president. With little hesitation, Trump flatly
stated that he would see what he could do. The very next day I saw
a news report in which he was talking about the importance of
developing Opportunity Zones.

Today, Opportunity Zones are enshrined in law and, at this
writing, $67 billion has been committed through opportunity
funds to flow into impovershed communities. Geographically,
according to the IRS, Opportunity Zones have been designated

in all fifty states, the District of Columbia, and five U.S. territories. Dear to my heart is the impressive list of zones all over my beloved state of South Carolina, including some impoverished areas where my own family is affected.

I am profoundly grateful to President Trump for listening to me and trying to better understand race relations in our country. But what about his simply and earnestly asking me what he could do to help? I cannot overlook the striking serendipity of the timing, that my team was right in the middle of pushing Opportunity Zones in the Senate tax bill, just when he asked!

Well, I think that remarkable coincidence drew its power from somewhere else—and from something other than my colorful socks. I believe it was providential.

A favorite saying of mine is one that was often used by Alex Haley, who in 1976 published *Roots,* a huge best-selling book that is considered the germinating force behind the explosion of interest in genealogy by the African-American community. At the height of his fame, Alex Haley would remind people:

"When you see a turtle sitting on a fence post, you can be sure he did not get there by himself."

Well, that's me. Whatever success I have enjoyed in both business and politics, I have been blessed by family, friends, business associates, and, most of all in recent times, my remarkable congressional staff. And my mission in life is to tell my story in a way that fosters confidence and understanding about the progress we have made as a country. Done effectively, the story can show all Americans these bedrock principles and how they can lift us all to a material and spiritual prosperity that will shine as a beacon for the rest of the world.

"To every kid growing up in poverty wondering if fitting in means dumbing down, the answer is no . . . to every single mom who struggles to make ends meet, who wonders if her efforts are in vain, they are not."

—FROM MY 2014 ELECTION NIGHT ACCEPTANCE SPEECH

CHAPTER 2

THE ROAD TO
OPPORTUNITY

"WHEN I GROW UP, I want to be a football player. The first thing I'll do is buy a house for my mom."

If we have heard it once, we have heard it a thousand times from so many kids growing up in impoverished neighborhoods. I was one of those boys with the dream. So many of us watch our moms and grandmothers leave early and come home late, sacrificing their own lives to put food on our table and clothes on our backs. Providing for mom and protecting her becomes the key motivation. When I was a kid, I was sold on the notion that a career in sports or entertainment would take me out of poverty and help me make my mom's dreams come true. And this was before professional athletes were paid the astronomical sums they receive today!

PASSION TO PLAY

I started playing little league football when I was seven years old, and my first team was the Cowboys. That began two of my long-term loves—football and the Dallas Cowboys. My athletic idol was

Tony Dorsett, a Hall of Fame running back for Dallas. I knew that if I could grow up and play as well as he did, then I could give my mom everything she had ever wanted.

Two goals began to fuse together: my passion to play in the National Football League, or at least be drafted by the Cowboys, and my passion to watch the moving truck move my mom into a nice house with a garage. High school football became a singular focus as I pursued those dreams. As is the case with many poor kids in the inner city, I felt that football was my ticket out of poverty and scraping to get by. It was my path into abundance and prosperity.

Chasing down the dream, I played on my high school team, and I had a very strong junior year personally. In fact, it would be twenty years before I learned how much of an impact that season made in my local community. Two decades later, I was on a men's retreat with a friend named Bob, who was also my roommate that weekend. We were talking football, and he went back to the glory years of his senior football season in 1982. Unbeknownst to him, that was my junior season. He started talking about that year and how his school, the Goose Creek Gators, had perhaps the best season in their school's history. For the first time ever, they had beaten the Summerville Green Wave, the number one team in the state. Then, he said, the next week they played Stall High School.

Bob told me all about this running back who ran over his team, eluding the defensive line and running over the defensive backs. He went on and on for fifteen minutes about this player, and how he could not remember his name but that he was a great player.

Finally, I could not take it any longer. I burst out laughing.

"What's so funny!" Bob demanded.

I jumped up on a chair, threw the Heisman pose at him, and

said, "I went left, I went right, and I ran all over you guys, because *I was that running back*!"

He literally pushed me off the chair and playfully threw me to the floor. He could not believe that number 44 from Stall High School was the guy standing in front of him now. It was one of the funniest moments I've ever had at a Christian men's conference. God must have a sense of humor to have made us roommates.

AIMING FOR THE TOP TIER

Back in the actual 1982, we finished my junior season with a losing record, a huge defeat of Goose Creek, and a lot of promise for a winning senior season. We had a solid backfield that would attract attention from many schools for a few of us, and we were excited about the upcoming season. I had garnered attention from some schools, but I wanted the experience and exposure from playing at a large Division I program.

The summer before the season started, I decided to team up with my college football friends who were succeeding at the next level. They would provide me with the necessary workout regimen and focus to capture the attention of the scouts, as well as solidifying the next step on my journey to secure my mom's financial future.

Day after day, practice after practice, I endured the unyielding tasks of evolving into a top tier college recruit. I was running the forty-yard dash faster and improving my weightlifting commitment, which in turn produced a stronger, healthier body and physique. In that summer between my junior and senior year, my mother bought a small house in Summerville outside of the Stall school border, which allowed me to play football for Summerville High School. I started August practices with the best focus, the greatest discipline, and the most energy ever.

Summerville was a football town with a powerhouse football program led by Coach John McKissick. Coach McKissick later became the winningest football coach in American history, winning more than 600 games for the Summerville High School Green Wave. I played running back, and at 5"11', 205 pounds, I was still fast enough to make the state championships in the 100 meters. Back in the early 1980s, a guy that big running that fast was pretty rare, and Coach McKissick helped feed my hopes of a football future. However, my heart remained at Stall High School, and I received permission to return to Stall and my teammates and friends. Back at Stall, we were certainly excited to take on the Green Wave later that season.

But for the time being, two-a-days continued. Water was a luxury. Wind sprints became our frenemies. And the hot, humid South Carolina Lowcountry weather was ever present. It was 80 degrees when we woke up, and everything just got hotter all day long. We were worked until we dropped, often in full pads. I particularly remember an exercise called the Monkey Roll, a drill for agility and conditioning, where basically you and two teammates alternated rolling on the ground and then jumping over each other. It was truly diabolical.

Two-a-days are grueling practices that include calisthenics, contact, and sweat-drenched drills. Working yourself and pushing to your limits was not uncommon during two-a-day practices, because it was in these types of practices that you forged the strength and commitment to turn a losing season into a winning one. We were stoked to be on the field even when we were nauseous, exhausted, and dehydrated.

On a morning toward the end of August and the beginning of the season, the routine continued as normal. I woke up blissfully unaware that it might be the last day of my football career or, even, the last day or my life. That day changed everything.

THE DAY WHEN EVERYTHING CHANGED

My mom and I shared a car in those days, and her workday started *early*. Unless I could convince one of my teammates to pick me up before practices and bring me home after, I had to get up as early as she did. Most mornings, I drove my mom to work so I could have the car for the day and make it to my two-a-days, which meant we had to be out by 6:15.

I was not then—and I am not now—a morning person, so this was a daily battle for us. I usually woke to the sound of my mother's voice around 6 a.m., calling me with the urgency of a single mother who depended on her teenage son for her ride to work. I heard a lot of "Timmy, I told you already to get your butt out of that bed!"

My older brother, Ben, was attending college at the University of South Carolina, meaning it was just my mom and me in the house. The car we shared was meaningful to us, in that it was my mom's first brand-new car. Back then, "brand-new" to us meant we bought a car with low mileage from a Budget Rental. It was a 1982 Toyota hatchback, and the sort of brown color you would associate more with a bad 1970s shag carpet than a car.

Those were long days for my mom and for me. She was typically working a sixteen-hour shift as a nurse's assistant, and then she came home to take care of our home as best she could. As for me, in addition to two-a-days, I was also working a few days a week at the movie theater until around midnight. I certainly took advantage of our free popcorn policy for employees, but the nights were still long. The last show typically started around 9 p.m., which meant we were left closing the theater at basically midnight. At best, that meant six hours of sleep.

We had also recently moved from my hometown of North Charleston, South Carolina, to a then-sleepy little town called Summerville, which doubled the commute time to downtown Charleston for my mother's job. So not only was my mom trying to wake me up to go to work, but I also knew that meant a forty-minute drive downtown, then back to North Charleston for a couple of brutal practices, and then to work at the movie theater.

This was all on top of the challenges you face growing up in a poor, single-parent household. My dad was not around, and on the rare occasions when I talked with him, I was reminded that I was glad he was not. My mom was working herself to the bone trying to keep a roof over our head, and that meant we did not get to see her as often as I think any of us would have preferred. In keeping with the transient nature of poverty, we had moved nearly half a dozen times in a decade. While I was publicly affable and loved to hear myself talk in school, there is no doubt that was covering quite a bit of anxiety and general unease about my place in the world.

So, it's safe to say, some mornings I was exasperated. A lot of mornings I was dead tired. And on this particular day, that led to me falling asleep behind the wheel.

I had dropped my mom off at work, and I was heading back up Interstate 26 toward Summerville. My eyelids felt like anvils, and I knew I was in trouble. I knew I had to do something to help me stay awake. I started to turn the heat all the way up, and then all the way back down. You know you are tired when your instinct includes turning up the heat in the sweltering heat of a South Carolina summer day.

When the heat made it worse, I opted for as cold as it could go. I switched over to the air conditioner, and turned it all the way up, and all the way back down. That worked for a few minutes, and then I had to figure something else out. I was traveling 65 miles per hour on the interstate when I started to roll the windows up and down. I cranked the radio. Blasting the music seemed like my last failed attempt. But a forty-minute drive is a long time to try to keep yourself awake, and I started nodding off.

I remember starting to drift between lines, and I recall snapping myself back awake a couple of times. But, eventually my body's demand for sleep won, and that was not good news for me—or for my mom's brand-new car.

My next memory is the sound of rubber tires kicking pebbles and gravel all over the place on the side of the road. As I started to go off the side of the road, the sound really grabbed my attention. I think we can all imagine what happens when a sixteen-year-old wakes up while driving 65 miles per hour on the side of the interstate—he panics! Instinctively, I simultaneously jerked the steering wheel and slammed on the brakes, causing my car to literally flip its way through morning rush hour. As my car tortuously made its way back through the eastbound traffic, the force and velocity of the car flipping brought me all the way across the westbound traffic as well.

One flip. Two flips. Three flips. I am honestly not sure how many, but it was more than enough. I flipped across four lanes of traffic, and my mom's brand-new car landed on its side, the roof caved in and the hatchback now just a part of the backseat. My back went through the windshield. I could have been thrown from the vehicle, but I stayed in the car only because I was able to hang on to the steering wheel. As the car came to rest on its side, I remember looking up to see the sky through a hole where a window used to be. My back and my legs were covered in blood and glass.

Then I heard someone speak.

A woman's voice said, "He's dead! I think he's dead!"

"I'm dead! I'm dead," I responded. I thought she was right.

I cannot remember who helped pull me from the wreckage, but I am so grateful for all the people who interrupted their early morning commute to help a kid in shock. I do remember lying on the side of the road with emergency responders buzzing around me, preparing to assist. I was on my side, looking up at the sky. I discovered, much to my chagrin, that there were shards of glass tucked into my gluteus maximus, aka my butt.

The highway patrolman approached me, and I just remember he seemed to be a mountain of a man. The officer seemed genuinely excited to see that I was, for the most part, still in one piece—perhaps even with a few extra pieces.

He kneeled down to talk to me and said, "Son, you've been in a terrible accident. You clipped one vehicle but no one else was injured."

Then he continued, "Your momma is going to be so happy you're alive."

I looked up, and I mustered the strength to tell him the truth. "Sir, you don't know my momma, because she is going to kill me!"

I begged him to call my aunt Nita instead. When she came to pick me up at the highway patrol office, I was only wearing one shoe. The other was still in the car somewhere. The officers gave my aunt two explicit instructions:

First, to take me to the hospital to get checked out, and second, to never let me see the car. I guess they did not think it would be healthy for me to see what I had survived. In fact, it took my mom and my aunt two days to get in the right frame of mind to go look at the car themselves. It had very nearly been the end.

The decisions that brought me to the side of that road, and

the choices that literally almost got me killed, were based on the belief that I had to physically work myself to the bone in order to change the future of my family. Without sports, how could a young black kid from a poor single-parent family ever take his life beyond the outskirts of the neighborhood?

That near-fatal crash helped reset my priorities. Today, decades later, the fact remains that many kids in low-income and distressed communities still feel the same hopelessness that I felt.

Oftentimes kids growing up in these areas are classified as "at-risk," but I prefer to call them "high potential" because there should be no limits on their future. I view it as my responsibility to find solutions that build up our communities. I want to show those kids, the ones who may believe the door to opportunity is locked, that they must muster up the intelligence, will, and drive to kick that door open.

Less than one percent of kids like me will ever make it out of poverty on a path paved with professional sports or entertainment. We have to find another way—not a continuation of the money-burning concepts introduced by President Lyndon Johnson's "Great Society" back in the sixties. I believe the best hope for turning poverty into prosperity is in the creation of Opportunity Zones all across the nation. We have worked long and hard to get Opportunity Zones established as part of our tax code, and they came into being as part of the Tax Cut and Jobs Act signed into law by President Trump in December, 2017. Now is the time to make them work.

The basic idea is to incentivize private capital investments in a way that encourages a long view as opposed to the short and quick turn-around on an investor's money. All of the underlying incentives relate to the tax treatment of capital gains as well as the longevity of the investor's stake in the particular qualified Opportunity Fund. The biggest upside is realized by the investor who holds his investment for ten years or more. Localities qualify as Opportunity Zones if they have been nominated for that designation by their state and that nomination has been certified by the United States Treasury Department, as specified in the law.

*　*　*

Since the creation of Opportunity Zones, I have visited more than a dozen states, seeing the innovative ideas and solutions that people are already creating to utilize them. Whether it's a rural county in Iowa, or a group of entrepreneurs in South Carolina, people are looking to make a difference in their communities as well as in their personal wealth.

More than 30 million people live in these zones, with incomes well below the average annual income for their states and in areas long forgotten by business and investors. That is changing now. In New Hampshire they are working on how to pair opioid recovery programs with workforce training programs to help battle the opioid epidemic. In Miami, youth centers and after-school programs are helping to keep more kids off the streets and give them a quality education. Erie, Pennsylvania, has seen a multimillion-dollar plan come together to invest in information technology and cybersecurity start-ups, while Chicago will see 3,300 units of affordable housing updated over the next couple of years. In South Carolina, we have a $54 million tech corridor coming to life, and in Newark, New Jersey, a $40 million fund has been started to provide housing for teachers.

And perhaps fittingly, given that conversation in the White

House, Charlottesville will see a mobile-home park converted into eight hundred units of affordable housing that will be made available first to current residents. These are concrete solutions to real problems, and the best part is these examples are just a sliver of the full potential of Opportunity Zones.

What warms my heart is to think about the individuals—and I mean the little boys and girls and their mothers and fathers and even their grandparents—who for the first time can see and feel small flickers of hope that things can get better. My dream is that they will begin to realize that their energy and skills are the most important tools for moving ahead and partaking of the prosperity that is achievable in our nation. My hope is that they will come to understand that progress—REAL progress—comes from what individuals do for themselves—and not what is simply handed to them.

OUT OF OBSTACLES COME OPPORTUNITIES

Literally anyone can start an Opportunity Fund, which is the actual financial mechanism that needs to be started in order to invest in the zones, from a small entrepreneur, to a town, to a billionaire philanthropist. (Some folks think billionaires are evil; I see them as hard-working people who, thanks to this new law, now have a huge chance to help reshape the future of communities across our nation.) You can help someone start a small business, invest in infrastructure projects, or start a larger business and create new jobs in an area where economic development announcements don't just fall off trees.

It is hard to overstate what this could all mean for folks living in these distressed communities. When you grow up hearing from the outside that your neighborhood is run-down or unworthy of other people's time, and see your friends head down the wrong path, it shrinks what you think is possible with your life. If there is no one around you succeeding, it is hard to keep your own belief in a brighter future for yourself.

The capital flowing through Opportunity Zones will certainly lead to big announcements and the creation of many new jobs. But the bigger impact will be in the slow drip of raising expectations and providing young kids like I was with role models and mentors punching through whatever glass ceiling was holding them down. Success can be contagious, and it can be as much about your mindset and belief as anything. Decades of neglect, bad policy, and lowered expectations have held us back for too long. For every big idea that comes out of Silicon Valley or midtown Manhattan, there could be a dozen being born at wobbly kitchen tables in rural Nebraska or under a leaky roof in Orangeburg, South Carolina. My dream is to see every single child and each family across this nation know that they have the opportunity to succeed, and that the American Dream is within their grasp.

I have grown fond of saying that out of obstacles come opportunities, from tragedy rises triumph, and struggle produces success. After a horrible car accident or significant loss, it is natural to wonder why you have been spared. But don't keep wondering for long! Any time is the best time to start turning those lemons into lemonade and building toward your highest goals. Yes, it takes fortitude—a fortitude seen throughout our amazing nation's history. For those willing to work smart and hard, the future has never been brighter.

For me, my mom's determination and vision provided significant wind beneath the wings of an unusual recovery from a near-death experience. My hope is Opportunity Zones will provide a necessary catalyst to help many who feel trapped with few resources to rise like the phoenix of old. I know that opportunity is the key to transforming lives—my own family lived through the struggle to find it.

"I'm not at a point where my grandfather was. He could say nothing. He had to eat his anger. Or the next generation, who harnessed their anger and led to marches. I'm on the inside track. I have a very different responsibility. It cannot be about me."

—SPEAKING WITH TIM ALBERTA IN THE MARCH/APRIL 2018 ISSUE OF POLITICO

CHAPTER 3

MY MOTHER'S AMERICAN DREAM

MILLIONS OF OUR fellow citizens are only a generation or two removed from poverty and hardship. I strongly believe that this commonality among Americans has been a key to holding our nation together through turbulent times. So many of us of all racial identities have parents or grandparents who grew up poor, whose job was driving the Dr Pepper delivery truck or toiling on a farm in the summer heat. We know their stories, and we are never far from those memories—those that are good as well as those that bring pain and uncertainty. This knowledge has helped us to understand the enduring faith and hope that hardships would lead to better lives for future generations. Always, to understand the value of where we are, we must hold on to our knowledge of others who have gone before us.

I have no doubt that I am living my mother's American Dream, and that dream would not exist if not for the hard work and dedication of her parents. To understand me, and where I'm coming from, you have to understand my mom. And to understand my mom, you have to learn about her father and her mother, Artis and Louida Ware.

MY GRANDDADDY, A LEGACY OF HARD WORK

My grandfather, Artis Ware, was born in 1921 in a small town called Salley in Aiken County, South Carolina. Today Salley (population around 400) has become known for the Chitlin Strut, a celebration of chitterlings, a very southern food that can, of course, be fried. The Strut brings together folks from across the community, and really is an amazing event, complete with a parade and all sorts of fun and dancing. But back when Granddaddy was born, things were very different.

Salley was the black community next to Wagener, a white town, so my grandfather's early life was defined by fierce segregation. When you grow up as a black kid in a small southern town, when you learn to always cross the street if a white person is approaching, your idea of what is possible stays very small—but even the frame of that "possible" was far advanced from that of our forebears. Granddaddy's hopes and expectations for what his life could be never got very big—though there is no doubt that he had them and held them quietly in his heart.

His childhood was further complicated by the loss of his mother when he was only six years old. At today's equivalent of first grade, Artis dropped out of elementary school to help on the farm and pick cotton. To be clear, stoop labor like picking cotton by hand is a terrible task. He had to fill bag after bag, ensuring the cotton was completely separated from seeds, soil, or other matter. Imagine a ten-year-old boy with the grizzled hands of an old factory worker, and you start to get a sense for just how difficult this work was. He did this for years and years.

During the times I knew him, Granddaddy did not speak often about the challenges he faced in those early years. But from the stories he told me in later years before he died, it was clear that he lived a subhuman life for too much of his youth and early manhood. In any case, young Artis's brutal toil developed a work ethic that would impact how he interacted with his family for decades—and how he framed the lessons he taught them.

My mom told me about the years when her family lived in the Daniel Jenkins Projects, a public housing facility, where families received government assistance to provide a place to live when they could not support themselves financially. Her parents were hardworking people. Her mama was a maid, and her dad was then a construction worker, so he was always moving from job to job looking for work. The pressure of poverty was ever present.

His struggles to be the man of the house were complicated by being a black man in the racially divided South, where finding work and keeping it could be two totally different challenges. As my grandfather spent so much time just looking for work, he became more volatile and disconnected from the family. Sometimes that meant he was pretty tough.

He faced some significant challenges, some because he was poor and more because he was black. But he never let those challenges break his spirit, and he held to the idea that his children and grandchildren had something better in front of them. He raised my mom with the belief that if she kept working, bigger things would come. As a kid, I knew that when my granddaddy spoke, I listened. My friends would later say the same thing about my mom.

As a youngster, my parents divorced and we—my mother, my brother, Ben, and I—had to move in with my grandparents. The five of us shared a two-bedroom, seven-hundred-square-foot house on a dirt road in an unincorporated settlement in Charleston County. My memories of our life in that tiny house are poignant—especially breakfast with our grandfather.

Ben and I would go into the kitchen, enjoying the aroma of coffee and biscuits. My grandfather made coffee in one of those old, gray coffeepots that looked like it would burn your hand off if you so much as looked at it wrong. As we had breakfast, Grand-daddy would be sitting by the window perusing the newspaper, slowly going from page to page, occasionally commenting on events.

He knew that education would be critical for our future success, and wanted to instill the importance of literacy and education not just with words, but with his actions. And he wanted us to see the importance of keeping up with the news around South Carolina and around the world.

Decades later, I learned the truth. While Granddaddy could see the newspaper's pictures and pick up a few words in headlines, he in fact never had the chance to learn to read. But, you see, he figured out a way to compensate for this shortcoming and teach Ben and me a powerful lesson.

Artis Ware lived to the age of ninety-four, which meant he got to see me become a United States senator. In his later years we still drove around in his Ford F-150 every Sunday. In fact, for most of that time he did the driving! But he lived all those years under the shadow of his life as a black man in the segregated South. On those Sunday drives, I would try to entice him to have lunch in one of the nice restaurants that we would pass. But no, he just could not be comfortable going into a place that had banished him for so long because of the color of his skin. The sting was as painful as ever. In all his years, I know of only three times that he ever had a meal in a restaurant.

But he was a physical powerhouse. One day when he was about eighty years old, my friend and campaign manager Joe McKeown and I went over to his house to chop some wood. Joe and I figured we could handle it, given that we both kept in shape by working out almost daily.

We started chopping, and while it was coming along, it wasn't easy. So, my grandfather walked over, took the axe, and split a piece of wood right down the middle on the first try. Then another, and another. At eighty! I believe humbling is the right way to describe this. Then, to top it off, he simply told us what we were doing wrong, showed us the right way, and then walked around to the backyard to finish what he was doing. Even with his advice, we still could not split them in one try! My grandfather was a man of strength, in every way.

MY GRANDMOTHER, A LEGACY OF FAITH

While Artis was no-nonsense and a little rough around the edges, my grandmother Louida was the spiritual matriarch of the family. Now, that is not to say she wasn't tough. My grandmother's dream was to go into nursing, but there were not many nurses who looked like her when she was growing up, and certainly not many opportunities to move forward. With less than a high school education, she could only find work as a maid, but always kept her dream of becoming a nurse.

As a maid, she would walk from Meeting Street in unincorporated Charleston County (now North Charleston) downtown every single day to clean houses. Sometimes she would catch a ride, but those times were few and far between. Let me tell you, walking a few miles round-trip through the Charleston heat in the summer—*and* working several hours a day cleaning houses—was not easy. And given the expectations of her generation, my grandmother had to cook and clean in other people's houses all day, and then come home and do the same at home—crammed into a two-bedroom house with her daughter and her two young sons.

In spite of the challenges in front of her, Grandmother was always happy, always encouraging. I liken our family to 2 Timothy

1, where the spiritual heritage of Timothy runs through his grandmother and mother, as does mine. Prayer, hard work, love, encouragement, and discipline, she was truly the embodiment of why we are here. Her prayer walk was so important to us, and she was responsible for what was the closest I have ever come to seeing a miracle.

It happened when I was about twelve and involved in a major football collision. When I was taken to the hospital downtown, the doctors determined that, among other things, I had fractured my neck. There was a crack in my vertebrae, and that most likely meant the end of my football career. The following week, my grandmother had a dream where she dropped a plate and it broke into two pieces. But, when she leaned over to start cleaning it up, the plate was whole again.

She told my mom about the dream, as she took it as a sign that my neck injury was healed, and insisted that I go back to the doctor to take another X-ray. Indeed, the second X-ray did not show the fracture. The medical team explained that the pressure had made things more difficult to see when I first came to the hospital. But we knew that my grandmother dreamed I was whole again, and I was back and ready to play football the next season! My grandmother's belief, her strength through tough times, has shaped our family forever.

Education was a driving force for my grandmother. I remember the graduation ceremony that she went through at a small church for Christian education. At the time, I could afford to help her buy a new dress to put underneath her robe, which was a small thing but meant a lot to both of us. It was a simple ceremony with about thirty people in attendance, but to her, it seemed like a stadium full of cheering fans as she walked across the stage to receive her certificate. She had worked hard and earned that certificate, and that meant so much to her. To me, it showed the powerful effect of recognition, something we all crave whether we admit it or not.

MY MOM, A LEGACY OF LOVE

My mom's life started with a humble beginning. Imagine, if you will, a little girl growing up in segregated South Carolina during the 1950s, with meager resources and too much responsibility. The second of five surviving children, she took on the responsibilities of being the cook, maid, and babysitter for the family.

She has always had this special quality of gravitating toward responsibility. This started when she was ten or eleven years old and her parents brought a new bundle of joy home in the package of her new little sister, Doretha. That age gap, as well as her own parents' efforts to keep a roof over their heads, meant my mom spent a lot of time with her little sister. Most fifteen-year-old girls probably would not want to hang out with their five-year-old little sister, but my mom understood what was placed on her shoulders, and met it head-on.

My mother inherited much of her parents' pain and misery, but she also inherited their work ethic and dreams for a better existence. In fact, my grandmother's dream to be a nurse, I believe is what motivated my mother to become a nurse's assistant for nearly fifty years. Maybe one of the reasons my mom refuses to retire, even though I've asked her to several times, is that she too is living her mama's American Dream.

My mom's drive, her motivation, and the love for serving others is hard to match. I call her my American hero, not just for everything that she has had to live through but for how she was able to utilize her struggles to drive her children to seek a brighter futures.

By the time she had my brother and me, my mom had already lived through a lot and learned too much about hard times. With a mixture of her natural tilt toward responsibility and my efforts to do whatever I wanted to do, she and I battled quite often when I was younger, whether over my poor grades, my yearning to be cool, or simply wanting a new pair of shoes we could not afford. Kids don't always understand what poverty truly means—when you are using the oven to heat the house in the winter, that likely means those new Converse high-tops are not coming anytime soon.

On the days when she worked a double shift, she would sometimes come home between shifts to check on Ben and me. Okay, mostly me. We were not allowed to go outside if she wasn't home, and if we did not answer the phone on the first ring, we would not need the phone to hear her voice. She would find us. I, of course, loved to challenge her rules, much to my backside's chagrin.

Thankfully, the rules and boundaries that my mom put on me when I was a kid were never crafted to limit what I could do, but rather to protect me from failing to reach my potential. She was working to keep me from killing myself, literally. As the family story goes, my brother and I were allowed to play in the front yard, but not go down the dirt to the pavement. The pavement was Meeting Street, a busy thoroughfare to this day. Me being me, I thought I would wander all the way down to the edge of the dirt and get as close to the pavement (and the cars) as possible. After a few brushes with death, she was forced to move the boundary back and introduce some penalties.

I know now that my mom was looking to keep me safe, not avoid having me do things that were annoying or made life harder for her. She always encouraged me; there was no raining on my parade, but simply efforts to keep me from falling into the traps that stop so many kids from reaching their potential—drugs, crime, jail, and even death.

No matter how much of a nuisance I was or how few material things we had, my mom never gave up. She never let me or my brother, recently retired as a command sergeant major in the U.S. Army, quit. She was not about to let our circumstances dictate the outcome of our lives. I can still hear her today telling us, "You are not going to be like the average person!"

We rarely got to go out for a meal, but when we did, mom made the most of it in terms of teaching us. She would have Ben and me get dressed up in our jackets and take us to the Pizza Inn on Rivers Avenue in North Charleston to share a few slices. She was trying to teach us how to behave and act properly, how to become the men she prayed we would become.

I am my mom's biggest fan, because for years I gave her the most to worry about. I cannot count the number of times I told her I was running away. I was a young kid who wanted more than we could afford, and I could not hide my frustration with our struggles. To this day, I find her tolerance of my challenges hard to fathom.

Today, Frances Scott, my mom, is still working in Charleston County, South Carolina. She's in her mid-seventies now, still giving her all. Family traditions started when I was just a youngster. When we no longer lived with my grandparents, we still spent every Sunday at my grandparents' house, and those Sunday dinners were amazing! Grandmom blessed us with delicious homemade biscuits, fresh veggies from my grandfather's garden next to the house they rented, and lemonade. That tradition lives on even after my grandparents have passed on. Every Sunday, my mom and I do something together. We enjoy lunch and/or a movie, and it is something I look forward to every single week.

THE BOND OF SHARED EXPERIENCE

Part of what binds us together as a nation is the shared experiences of our pasts. Even if you were raised in the South, growing up on a farm, you had something in common with the factory worker's kid growing up outside Detroit.

I vividly remember how when we were allowed to watch television, we had just three channels to choose from. There were no remote controls; in fact for my mom and grandparents Ben and I were the remotes. Sometimes the knob you had to turn to change the channel would break, and we would have to find the pliers to stick into the front of the TV to do it.

Thankfully, there were only three channels to change between with the pliers. Now I recognize that just having those three channels meant that most Americans were operating from the same set of facts. That is not to say that different opinions were not shared, but there was a much higher premium on news than opinion, almost as if we were forced to make up our minds for ourselves instead of having them made for us.

This, more than anything else, is part of what is being stripped away from us today. We do not watch the same television channels, and we do not read the same newspapers. The common ground of the Bible that sustained generations of Americans is increasingly diminished. Heck, there's plenty of evidence that people are even physically moving to neighborhoods where most of the residents more closely align with their political views. As media silos fracture our understanding of others, and social media serves only to reinforce what we already agree with, we lose the great value of shared experiences.

The absence of shared experiences leads to so much misunderstanding and divisiveness. From that often comes an almost irrational emphasis on "winning" at any cost. In the interest of "winning," we are actually allowing ourselves to be torn apart. It is a relentless cycle that threatens to break our nation apart. Many good women and men, including my good friend Trey Gowdy, have decided to leave politics because of this win-at-all-costs mentality. Winning at all costs only guarantees losses we can ill afford as a nation.

But I am still brimming with hope for us. And that hope stems from one fact, and my own experience. The fact remains that we have made so much progress. Just in my lifetime, black people were hosed down in the streets of Birmingham and beaten on the Edmund Pettus Bridge in Selma, Alabama. That is unimaginable today. There have been some profound changes for the better in the area where my grandfather was raised. Aiken County is also right across the Savannah River from Augusta, Georgia, where more than seventy years after my grandfather was born, a young black man would walk down the stately fairways of Augusta National Golf Club and win the Masters. The significance of Tiger Woods's white caddie carrying his bag of thousand-dollar golf clubs less than fifty miles from where my black grandfather had to fill and carry bags of cotton is certainly not lost on me.

This dynamic is also what made it so special for me to receive an energetic reception at Wagener-Salley High School in 2016. While I am sure there are normal high school issues, there was no animosity, none of the expectation-killing vitriol that drove the early part of my grandfather's life. To be able to tell those kids that literally anything is possible, that my family went from cotton to Congress starting right here in Salley, South Carolina, was truly special.

Don't get me wrong, there are still terrible and unacceptable things that happen.

As a whole, though, impressive progress has been made since 1965. Imagine a restaurant or a public square attempting today to have a whites-only water fountain, or black students not being allowed to attend the University of Mississippi. We have made much progress.

As I mentioned in the first chapter, one of my most meaningful experiences is when I traveled to Selma, Alabama, with my friend congressman John Lewis of Georgia, one of the most eloquent and distinguished voices in the civil rights movement. To see the Edmund Pettus Bridge, to feel the same air that those folks felt as police descended on them simply for having the gall to march for voting rights—that experience will change a person forever. And to do so with a friend like John Lewis was even more powerful. I stood in front of this bridge where fifty years ago I probably would have been spit on, and thought of all the sacrifices made before us. Some were made by those knowing the danger they were putting themselves in, courageous men like Dr. Martin Luther King or Medgar Evers, and some by kids like Emmett Till who had no idea what their lives would come to mean. Without them, who knows where I might be today, but I am pretty certain it would not be the United States Senate.

I remember the first time I visited John Lewis's office after being elected to Congress. I was in awe at the history on the walls, pictures of him on the bridge with Martin Luther King and so many others. I asked for some advice from this man. A man who had lived his whole adult life as a Democrat, fighting for the next generation to be able to reach higher—a man who had been beaten unconscious by police and jailed . . . And here's what Congressman John Lewis told me: "Never, ever, become bitter."

That was so powerful, so awesome to hear, that even as a natural optimist I felt even more optimistic about where we are going. While some challenges persist, the wisdom and courage of Congressman Lewis—as well as my own life experiences—lead me to believe that we can come back together.

My mom taught me that no matter what was in front of us, we could make our own future no matter how dark the present. And I believed her, because I knew our family's history. This is the benefit of shared history: to understand the value of where we are, we must hold in our hearts the works and experiences of those who have gone before us.

"My life is a testament to God's love, a mother's love, and the love of my mentor."

—FROM A A SPEECH I GAVE ON THE SENATE FLOOR IN JULY 2016

CHAPTER 4

SURVIVAL

LOOKING BACK TO those very early years, what now seem to be deprivations were not that for a happy child living in a warm cocoon of family and friends. I had a big brother and a doting mother, as well as grandparents who thought I was a special little kid. All of my people worked. The food was good, and I don't recall ever going to bed hungry. My father was the boss, just as he should have been.

Whatever stress was in our home was not seen by my little-boy eyes, or heard by my innocent ears. During the earliest years in Charleston, I was a happy kid. So it's not surprising that out of this warm security arose a confidence that our sudden move to the great Midwest was an exciting prospect. Indeed, we were moving to a place called Scott Air Force Base, and my brother and I had no doubt that the whole shooting match was named for us!

My father had joined the U.S. Air Force, and his first posting was to Scott AFB near St. Louis. I was around four years old when we left warm and sunny South Carolina to meet Old Man Winter—a terrible and most memorable shock to my whole system. In more ways than the weather, this move was just the beginning of my family's toughest challenges.

Surviving the cold for a young kid from the South was difficult, but it paled beside what lay ahead: the breakup of our family. I didn't really understand what was going on with my parents, but there was a gloom at hand that told me something had gone very wrong in my parents' marriage. Simply put, we had been happy in Charleston, and we were very unhappy in St. Louis.

My dad's life was colored by many challenging events, from having a mother who lost eleven out of fourteen children, to missing the day I was born because he was on special assignment for the military in Thailand during the Vietnam war. My dad and I never even talked about Vietnam or the loss of his eleven siblings until his seventy-fifth birthday! In learning about these things that shaped his life, and thus my own, I am getting to know my dad as an adult in a way that I never knew him as a kid.

The story of our military adventure, I am told, starts at our namesake base in Illinois where, early on, I began to establish my reputation as mischevious—mainly because of my relentless curiosity. I was about four or so when I was left in the hands of a babysitter. My brother, Ben, always a better-behaved and focused child, played happily as I found entertainment in a more mischievous way. My dad was a smoker and had a cool collection of lighters. That evening while he and my mom had dinner at the noncommissioned officers' club, I decided to play with his lighter shaped like a little play gun. Did you know you can run your fingers through a flame and not get burned? Well, I do. I learned it that night. However, the key is to not stop moving your fingers because at that point you will feel the heat.

Well, once my fingers were singed, I no longer wanted to play with the lighter. I yelled and threw it on the bed. Yep, fabric is flammable. In a panic, the babysitter called my parents at the NCO and the fire truck showed up at the house to help put the small fire out. Needless to say, my parents were frightened and furious. The good news for me was that they were so angry that I didn't get a spanking because the family rule is you never touch a kid in anger! I can honestly say I was very thankful for family rules.

After our time in Illinois, the Air Force apparently decided that was not cold enough for us, and my dad was sent to Kincheloe Air Force Base in Michigan. Now, southern Illinois was a bit chilly, but Michigan is downright cold. That isn't news to people from Michigan, but it certainly was to a six-year-old from North Charleston. I definitely thought I wouldn't survive the winter. It felt like if you breathed too hard your lungs might freeze if your lips didn't beat them to it. So, imagine my surprise, moving from a place where if the weather forecast says it might snow a quarter inch in two days everything shuts down, to where we had to go to school in several inches of snow and temperature of minus-15 degrees! We would be kept inside to play in our basement because it was so cold we were not allowed (and did not want) to go outside.

The Upper Peninsula was about as polar (pun intended) opposite as you could get from Charleston. I think the next time I enjoyed winter weather was when it snowed in Charleston in 2017 and a neighbor hooked a boogie board up to a golf cart and pulled people down the street. There may or may not be video of this on the internet.

Kincheloe was a relic of the Cold War and closed permanently in 1977 (which was not long after we were stationed there). My dad had done well in the Air Force, and this was another step up the ladder for him. Although it was just the second time we had moved, for all we knew there was a lifetime of base-hopping ahead of us.

* * *

While in Michigan, I missed my grandparents, my friends, and South Carolina. I knew I was miserable, but what I didn't know was that when we moved to Michigan, it was the last time we would move together as a family. And that was worse pain than any minus-10-degree day could inflict.

My dad seemed to roll right along with the move, but for the rest of us it was much more of a struggle. I remember, perhaps not 100 percent accurately, tromping my way to school through the backyard in the snow that seemed to come up to my ears (actually, it was likely only halfway up my galoshes). Snowball fights in the yard with my brother were really fun but not for long.

As you can tell, I am not a fan of the cold. In addition to the cold, I was growing up in a house with a dad who was tough and unyielding, fitting the stereotype of some military men. He and my mom seemed unhappy and I didn't understand what was happening, though I'm sure my older brother, Ben Jr., had more of an inkling. It is hard to put into words how seeing my unhappy parents fight made me feel as a kid, and the way it changed my perception of the world. Given the choice, we would all love to live in a happy, sitcom family full of laughs and high-fives, but that's just not how life always works.

I wondered if it was my fault. What had I done? I would sit on the edge of my bed thinking, practically begging for someone to tell me. Was I too loud? Did I say something wrong? Of course, being so young I was not able to process my tumultuous relationship with my father. He was the cool dad one minute, cooking us pancakes for a family breakfast on Sunday morning, and then angry and abrasive the next moment.

One day, my brother and I were out on the base and got into a scuffle with some of the neighborhood kids. As I remember it, a few kids surrounded my brother and me after school, and we were about to start swinging. My brother was always the intellectual one, and I am sure he deduced that the consequences for fighting would not be worth the sensation of success. So, while I fought to hold down the fort, my brother ran home to seek adult supervision. My dad's reaction? He disciplined my brother for leaving me back there on my own.

Over the years, I've tried to process things I heard as a child, and determine whether my memories are actually memories or just stories told repeatedly that have led me to construct my own mental images. Reconnecting with my dad took years, decades really. The older I got, the more I realized the damage inflicted did not make me angry or sad. It simply made me disinterested. If we talked, great. If we did not, that's fine, too. However, that is now the perspective of a man in his early fifties, not a seven-year-old kid who just wanted everything to be okay.

I remember the first time I really visited my dad after the divorce. I was twenty-three years old and a college graduate. That was a full sixteen years after my parents split. I am certainly glad to have had the chance to meet my brother Earl, his soon-to-be wife, and later, his two sons, and to learn a little more about my family on my father's side. Earl is now retired from the Air Force as a full-bird colonel, and a graduate of the United States Air Force Academy where he played football. He is married to his lovely wife of more than twenty-five years, Mel, with two sons of their own, Braeden and Caiman. Earl was raised by my dad from age five. Interestingly enough, I think Earl had the personality and disposition to blossom where he was planted with my dad.

I remember the story he told at my dad's seventy-fifth birthday party about growing up with my dad. He talked about how he was all county in football and won awards like player of the week and many other accolades. Dad would encourage him by saying his older brother (me) had it harder, and needed to ride his bike to practice while Earl was able to drive in a nice car. Earl took the ribbing well, and became an even better football player than I was.

He also found dad's sternness challenging but used it to become a better person. Some wilt while others blossom. It's taken many years for all of us to talk through the differences and the challenges of our upbringing, but we find new strength and greater understanding by opening up. In the same way I have benefited from those who went before me and built an amazing heritage in my family, we as a nation need more family conversations! America's future benefits from a strong, honest, and clear dialogue about who we are and the struggles of the past.

As an adult, I can now see how many goals and points of pride—some contradictory—can exist in one's mind at the same time. Many of us struggle with this personally, as does the nation itself. We are proud of what we stand for but in some instances, not so proud. It can prove difficult for us to have real conversations regarding the dark times in our nation's history, just as it is a challenge for me to really consider the effects of personal trauma such as my family splitting up.

It can be easier to try to avoid the contradictions altogether, or attempt to lessen the impact of what occurs. America cannot afford to continue doing that. While I do not believe we can blame all of our issues on what occurred in the past, we need to have a true reckoning with what those tragic times really meant. Whether it's the Trail of Tears, or slavery, or Japanese internment camps during World War II, there are long-lasting scars on the psyches of certain groups of people in this country. And when we come together to solve problems, it is absolutely necessary for us to consider their frames of reference even if it makes us a little uncomfortable.

The day my parents' relationship ended for good, Ben Jr., my mom, and I got in the car and drove home to South Carolina and my grandparents. All we took with us were our clothes. The chasm between my dad and me continued to grow, mainly because our infrequent communications were incredibly negative, and left me feeling worse about my predicament and myself. What had started as a winter I wasn't sure I would survive turned into one my family didn't. My foundation was crumbling, and our future was uncertain.

In my worst fears, right now America is facing the moment when our foundation is crumbling. People are less concerned with what our founding documents actually say than with what they want them to say. We are so worried about being right, we are forgetting we need to work together to survive.

My family figured that out. We came together. My mom worked and worked and worked, and we made it through as a new family, perhaps smaller in number, but bigger in heart. It took me until I was thirty to really come to grips with my dad, and even longer to forgive him.

However, beyond the tragedy of my family falling apart, and all of that Michigan snow, was a culture change that was to endure for the rest of my life. So often, perhaps even too often, our world-view is shaped at a very young age. One of my fondest memories on the military base was how important it was to acclimate to a new environment. Back at home in South Carolina we played with only black kids and in only black neighborhoods, without exception.

My first foray in a diverse culture was on that military base and as uncomfortable as the cold was, this new culture of diversity, of inclusion, fit me like a glove. I found myself drawn to kids of different backgrounds. As I look back now, perhaps the most important discovery at Kincheloe was the important role, the paradigm shifting experience, of being embraced as just another kid on the military base. The beauty of base-hopping is that your friends were the kids on the street, black, white, or brown. It was simply one neighborhood. This left an indelible impression on me. I remember one little girl who was half French and half black, and she was my first crush. I learned very quickly that if you treated everyone the same, regardless of backgrounds or skin color, very often you would find that they would treat you in the same fashion.

This is a lesson that has stuck with me all my life. People often ask me why I never joined the Congressional Black Caucus. Truth is, it is a form of setting ourselves apart, and my prayer is that we work toward becoming more inclusive—not exclusive. For sure, there was a time and place when it was important for black Americans to form groups in order for our voices to be heard, but I think it is important for us to move into the mainstream as conditions change. But for me, from the early age of six or seven, my world was always diverse. It's where I found my true fit. I would learn to fight for people of varying backgrounds because I felt like it was my responsibility, my job; it was as if the good Lord gave me a passion for protecting and seeking justice for all people.

I discovered a lot about myself as an Air Force kid, and I really think between athletics and the military our nation has made more progress on the issues of race and inclusion than any other institutions in our country. My hope for our country was born on an Air Force base. One American family, one American patchwork quilt. The patches are black and white, red and brown, bound together by the threads of democracy, the hope of freedom. My passionate pursuit to bridge the gap and to bring people together was ignited by the ease with which I interacted with kids from all over the country.

I reject the concept that we are better apart for it is obvious there is one God and he has put us together for a greater purpose. We are better together! I love the story of the leader of a Black Lives Matter event who was conducting a protest outside of a Trump rally that was not yet underway. He was somehow invited on the stage of the rally. Now, common sense would tell you not to invite the opposition into the Trump gathering, much less onto the stage or, even worse, giving him time to talk to your supporters. But that's exactly what happened. For the next fifteen minutes or so the Trump crowd listened as he articulated his position, and peppered throughout his comments were standing ovations when the crowd responded to the statements with which they agreed.

That's the America that makes me so proud. Even when we sharply disagree, we can still find a way to get up, cover the ground, and make progress. If the Black Lives Matter leader and the organizer of the Trump rally can figure it out, so can we.

How did they figure out how to make that happen? I think the answer is kind of simple. I learned it a long time ago. If you don't question the intentions or motives of people who disagree with you, you are in a far better position to hear them out. It's when we question their motivation that we make enemies out of the opposition. It is hard to insult people into changing their minds.

Universal agreement cannot be necessary for two sides to be friends. It's the things we have in common that bind us, not the things on which we disagree. I learned a tough lesson about that my junior year in high school. My friend was taking me over to his house to hang out for a bit. He lived in a dream neighborhood! Individual houses, sidewalks, even a driveway and a garage. He might have taken for granted how much of a blessing it was to have his own yard, but as an apartment dweller for the vast majority of my life, I always felt like kids who lived in houses were just a little better off or just a little better than me because they had so much.

My friend told me that I would never make as much money as his dad or his family. We were talking about our future ambitions, and he could not even imagine me having such an unrealistic goal as to earn an income in the same hemisphere as his dad! I recall the feeling in my stomach as he laughed at me. To be fair, he was comparing his life to mine. I was comparing his outsides to my inside.

We went around and around that day and it could have easily been a breaking point for our friendship. Finally, I said to Lincoln, "so you think it's impossible for me to earn a similar income as your dad?" He hemmed and hawed but finally said he thought it would be a challenge for me to get there. I asked him if he thought it would be as challenging for him to achieve his dad's income, and he said not as much, but he would have to work hard to make it.

What I realized in that moment was that his view was blinded by my circumstances and mine was emboldened by my inner vision. I continued the conversation and landed a few important points. First was the old adage, don't judge a book by its cover. Second, even friends with good intentions may see you from an inferior position. Finally, the value you have starts within and grows out.

We can disagree without being disagreeable, and seek to understand without forcing our own opinions on others. We saw it after the tragedy of Mother Emanuel Church in Charleston, and we often see it in the wake of other senseless horrors. America comes together when it looks like we could splinter apart. Moving forward, we must focus on working better together so that we are more readily prepared to do so when tragedy strikes.

Perhaps one of my greatest lessons about learning to disagree without being disagreeable comes from two friends, Ed and John. These men have much in common. They are both African-Americans, both residents of the South Carolina Lowcountry, and both officers in their local NAACP branches. As a youngster, I grew up as a member of the NAACP. Ed was our neighbor, and at the time, the president of the North Charleston branch. He was always a smart man who understood the importance of being a role model to young boys in the neighborhood, and he could fix anything.

Ed would constantly fix our cars for the price of parts when we couldn't afford to pay him for his labor. He was an ace mechanic. We've all heard stories about how you can hold anything together with duct tape—it's a southern tradition. Well, Ed was our human duct tape, making everything last just a little bit longer than it should. He seemed to stitch things together effortlessly.

When you're driving used cars, you're typically driving someone else's problems. I remember one such car was the Gremlin. There's a high probability that most of you have never heard of a Gremlin unless you saw *Anchorman 2,* and if you haven't, I hope you realize how blessed you truly are! Well, we drove one and it was a horror show! The one thing that car did really well was spend money, and not on gas. It was always broken. We could depend on it to be undependable. But Ed was ready to hop in there and save us over and over. As a master mechanic, he was able to put that Gremlin back on the road time and time again. Fortunately for us, and probably for him, we finally were able to get rid of the Gremlin and get another amazing used car.

Ed and his wife, Betty, lived around the corner in the same apartment complex and he provided me with much-needed male leadership. Today our politics cannot be more different. But I've still called on Ed to help fix my car or someone else's car. The answer is still the same, "Where did it break down?" And, "I'll be there in about thirty minutes."

These days Ed definitely lobbies me on a multitude of issues. Sometimes we find common ground, but most of the time we don't. One thing we do have in common is an affection that transcends politics. I can count on Ed because he is a good person. He is an advocate for the poor, a strong role model for young boys and young men, and a man who's been married to the same woman for more than forty-five years.

John is the vice president of another Lowcountry NAACP. My friendship with John started after I was an elected official. We don't talk about specific issues and politics, but John has on occasion called me to share his disappointment in a vote or his encouragement for getting it right. Once again, we don't see eye to eye on every political issue, but the one thing we both share is a strong desire for the truth.

The thing that bonds us together is John's faith. Every day, without fail for the last several years, John has sent me a daily prayer every morning at about 6 a.m. He has been so consistent with sending the prayer that if it's after 9 a.m. and I have not received it, I text him to ask for it. That's only happened about three or four times in the last few years. He is disciplined about the responsibility of sharing good news and the light even on dark days. John has critiqued my decisions and performance, but I have not found him to be harsh. I can't tell you how much I appreciate having someone who disagrees with me, at times vehemently, but

I can still talk to him about why he thinks I'm wrong and where we can find common ground.

John and I have talked about many issues, some of them being constituent services issues. This is a place where I find common ground with many of my friends who are liberals. When you call our office, we never ask you about political affiliation or anything else. We ask how can we serve you, and then we go about getting the job done. It's a blessing to walk into a restaurant in South Carolina and have someone walk up to me and thank me for the way that my office handled their constituent concern. I smile and remind them that the goal of being an elected official isn't to first represent my party affiliation, but first it's to represent my families—my South Carolina family and my American family. I do so with great joy! John has sent me several constituent service cases, and so far, he seems to be pleased with our success at solving the problems or at least honestly telling the constituent that it is beyond our reach.

Both these men have taught me how to disagree without being disagreeable, but more important, they've taught me how to respect people who don't agree with me and remain friends. I can count on both of those men to be there when I need them. I won't promise you that they both vote for me—well, I hope that they do, but I know that if all the chips are down and I need a ride, my car fixed, or help with a life issue, they will be there for me.

That's the story of America. It's not about our resources, not about our wealth, not about our race even; it's about each other. We share a common bond that grows stronger when we put our own priorities second to what's really important—nourishing the spirit of the American family.

"If you learn from defeat,
you haven't really lost."

—Zig Ziglar

CHAPTER 5

SECOND CHANCES AND NEW OPPORTUNITIES

SOMETIMES CONGRESS CAN feel a lot like high school. There's bad behavior, rumor mongering, and gossip. There are comparisons and competitions. There are the cliques of rich kids and the poor kids, and there is every possible stereotype you would find in movies like *The Breakfast Club* and *High School Musical*. If you come to Congress as a shrinking violet, you are going to have a tough time adjusting. Much like high school, though we all seem to be here for the same purpose, we don't come at it the same way. And we don't always like each other.

I played football in high school and college, and a lot of my life's lessons seem to come back to scrimmage lines and end zones, coaches and plays. The football field has always been a place where I seemed to learn best. Even today, I find myself taking notes during football games and movies about this ultimate team sport, because there's something about the challenge, the pain, and the sense of accomplishment that embeds the lessons of life deep in my heart and mind in a way that I never forget.

In the movie *Remember the Titans*, there is a scene where a black player and a white player are trying to learn how to play as a team. They each question the other's commitment, and they end up challenging each other in aggressive ways on the field. I lived this scene in real life, at Stall High School, between one of our defensive ends and me.

As a running back, I took great pleasure in running with my head down and barreling through a defensive player. As a defensive end, my fellow player found great delight in making sure that I gained as few yards as possible. I would come running around the corner as he was steaming toward me, and neither one of us was going to give an inch. We locked helmets time and time again, and we kept barreling after one another—even after the whistle blew. During one practice, we had to be separated by our coaches. That's when I knew this defensive end and I would be facing off all year.

Our dislike for one another did not stop at the end of practice. We did not speak to each other when we passed in the hallway, even as we wore our jerseys on game day. Even though we were teammates, we challenged each other like hardened rivals, even enemies.

During the fall of my junior year, we played against the Goose Creek Gators, and let me tell you, they had a reputation for being a tough—and sometimes nasty—team. Today I still have a scar on my right wrist from a Gator's face mask sticking into my arm. The week before playing us, they had defeated our major rival, Summerville, a school that had won multiple state championships. Goose Creek was not simply aggressive; they were ruthless, relentless, and downright mean—and they certainly intended to keep on winning.

My team, the Stall High School Warriors, was the underdog, and we played our hearts out. As we neared the end of the second quarter, those undefeated Gators began to realize they had clearly underestimated us. Their perfect season and their top ranking seemed to be slipping away with each play. Never let your guard down against the Stall High Warriors!

The clock ticked down, and the players for Goose Creek became more aggressive. I vividly remember running a sweep to the right with linebackers closing in and tackling me to the ground. As I stood up, I felt someone kick me in the side and push me back down to the ground. They didn't care if they broke a rib, bruised a kidney, or punctured a lung. The Gators wanted to win, and they were determined to take me down.

As I lay pinned under this pile of Gators, I saw a player in a Stall High School Warrior jersey. He came to my rescue, plowing through our opponents, and throwing each one of the Goose Creek guys off me. When I looked up and saw my defender, I couldn't believe who it was. I had been rescued by that defensive end who had been my nemesis, my rival on my own team.

That was my first understanding of teamwork, of setting aside differences for the sake of the common goal. He and I had hated each other for weeks, on and off the field, but when the moment mattered most, he became my ally. After all, we were on the same team.

AMERICAN EXCEPTIONALISM

That night on the football field is not so different from what we may be experiencing today. Our nation has faced racial tension, but our greatest assets arise from our people from every tribe. Our uniform is not worn over our shoulders; it's buried in our hearts. We must call upon our better angels to overcome the silos of tribalism. I came from a place where racial tension was abundant, where tribes formed consistently. And yet, I am optimistic because I have watched us overcome many of those divisions, and I lived through the pain and triumph of that journey. We may challenge each other when times are good, but under pressure, we rally to each other's defense to protect each other.

As American people, we rally not only for the ones we love, but also for the ones we don't love. We even rally for the ones we've never met. This is what I consider true American exceptionalism, this willingness to sacrifice for others. We rise to the occasion because we are exceptional. It is incumbent upon each of us to tell the story of America, which includes the story of you, me, and millions of others. As a nation, our story and our journey are filled with obstacles, challenges, and impediments. But as we face these, we shine the brightest. We show the world that America is different.

In the early 2000s, I spent four years on a hospital foundation board, helping to raise money for patients who could not afford the care they needed. I was amazed by the philanthropic efforts of people and communities that made donations anonymously. Many of our largest gifts came from anonymous donors, because their goal was to improve the prospects of a healthy community, not to gain glory for themselves.

Hospital foundation boards are quite interesting, because some require each member to contribute five thousand dollars to serve on the board. I had served on other boards previously without a minimum financial contribution, so this requirement caught me by surprise. I thought it was hilarious that I needed to pay money to volunteer my time and expertise. What I learned along the way, however, was far more valuable than my resources, be they time or money. I learned about what makes America great. It really does come down to what makes us good: a willingness to do for others with no expectation for a return.

Our campaigns exceeded millions of dollars donated by local folks because of their strong desire to improve the health outcome of someone that they would never meet. A local philanthropist, George, is well known to have contributed a large amount of money to his community through hospitals, the United Way, Red Cross, and many other organizations.

During one of the floods over the past five years in South Carolina, I had a previously scheduled political fund-raiser on the calendar. Obviously, we were going to cancel it, but then we came up with a better idea. Instead of a political fund-raiser, we decided to create an event to help our communities who have been inundated by floodwaters. Our plan was to donate all the money raised to the Red Cross. I was on the stage encouraging the attendees to support the community by giving what they could and getting involved in helping their neighbors.

I turned to the crowd, and I raised my voice loud like a preacher winning souls. "We only need one person to do all they could do! Isn't there just one person who will come up and join me in contributing to our efforts?" I ran across the stage, preaching to people about donating to the Red Cross and changing lives. As I was finishing up, George said he would make a contribution. I was thrilled, and I asked how much he was willing to pledge. George said, "Fifty!"

I said, "Well, fifty dollars is a great start," and he just looked at me with that small grin on his face.

I decided to up the ante, and I said, "Fifty thousand dollars?" George looked up to the ceiling, and he gave me the thumbs-up. I could not believe my ears, that he had decided to invest $50,000 to help people struggling through our community. This was the embodiment of American exceptionalism—to come to the rescue of people you have never met—and might never meet.

I love the giving pledge, where wealthy Americans give more than 50 percent of their income to charities. These charities will undoubtedly help people of different races, different backgrounds, and varying socioeconomic situations.

One of the most beautiful examples of American exceptionalism has unfolded in an organization called Proverbs 22:6, a program that serves the families of those who are incarcerated. Statistics have shown that 70–80 percent of children whose parents are in prison will end up in prison themselves, but Proverbs 22:6 has stepped in to turn those numbers around, one family at a time. The nonprofit is named after the verse in Scripture that says, "Start children off on the way they should go, and even when they are old, they will not turn from it." Embracing this verse as a mission statement, Proverbs 22:6 has set the goal to keep one million children out of prison.

The founder moved to America from India, and within his first month in the United States, he was robbed at gunpoint. Such an encounter often causes people to become hardened and resentful, but this man became better instead of growing bitter. He began to study the patterns of criminals, an interesting choice for someone who had just been the victim of criminal activity. As he learned about these individuals, he discovered that what they really needed was rehabilitation. He recognized that the connection between parent and child is one of the broken links of recidivism and rehabilitation programs, so he founded a nonprofit organization that reconnects these parents with their children.

Proverbs 22:6 encourages the incarcerated parent to become a part of their children's lives and helps define their roles and responsibilities to their child. It attempts to restore the foundation of the family by mending the relationship between father or mother and child through engaging in restorative activities. It seeks accountability, offers mentoring, and teaches the incarcerated parent how to encourage their child. The organization even provides financial support for postsecondary education, knowing that the child's best chance at not following their parents' footsteps is to get a good education. This issue affects every American, since our country spends $74 billion incarcerating people. (That's a B-as-in-boy *billion dollars* annually.) If private sector programs can impact these numbers, it breaks the cycle of generational incarceration and benefits everyone.

I spent several hours touring state facilities to watch and learn from the program. At one male facility, I served the inmates meals and enjoyed conversations with many of them. This experience was moving, particularly as I watched the fathers prepare to meet their kids. Most of the experiences were beautiful reunions, but there were some tension-filled moments when the children could not bear meeting their dads. The children would simply not show up. The fathers were devastated. When someone is in prison, the ripple effect is fierce among the people who loved them most.

But Proverbs 22:6 seeks to serve and meet the needs of the whole family, giving each child, mother, and father time to heal, process, forgive, and try again. Very often, within a few months if not a couple of weeks, the dads and the kids are reunited once more. This reunion starts the process of moving the men to a place of reflection and change. Even the most hardened inmates seem to soften as they come face-to-face with their own blood.

What is the secret sauce to his program? Love! The inmates experience the unconditional acceptance that comes from their children.

This program has become such a success that the recidivism rate of folks that enter their program is one of the lowest in the country, averaging less than 10 percent, compared to the average federal recidivism of 77 percent. From my efforts in criminal justice reform, I have seen that it's not the government that runs the best recidivism and reentry programs. The programs that do the most fantastic work are those founded in the hearts and minds of individuals who now feel compelled to provide resources, training, or opportunities for people as they reenter society. When we give people our all, in return they often give us their all.

OPPORTUNITIES START EARLY

I can personally speak to the power of interventions in the lives of children. Without some powerful people to get me on track, I wouldn't have finished high school. After my dad left, I dove into a years-long game of trial and error, wondering just how far I could push the rules, both at school and at home. At home, I pushed both my mother's and my brother's patience as far as it could go. At school, I found that I enjoyed being the class clown and football star far more than working hard and doing my schoolwork. That sort of attitude led me to basically flunk out of the ninth grade.

For starters, after my parents divorced, I failed English and Spanish, and when you fail both English and Spanish, no one calls you bilingual. They call you bi-ignorant because you can't speak any language! To compound the problem, I also failed World Geography and Civics. That's right, ladies and gentlemen, I am a United States senator who once failed the study of politics.

I will say that after a few years in the United States Senate, after knowing friends and colleagues on both sides of the aisle, I now suspect I am not the only one who didn't do so well, either. One of the most damaging decisions of the last fifty years is the Budget and Control Act (BCA) of 2011, when we used our military as a political pawn to reach a budget deal. Coupled with President Obama announcing a ten-year, half-trillion-dollar cut to our military, this represented nearly a $1 trillion drop in funding and a mass interruption of our military priorities. Add to that the concept of sequestration, the basic elimination of sorely needed funds until we were able to get the budget passed. From my view, this led to the crippling of our military priorities. That's a classic example of the failure to understand the importance of civics.

Or consider the poor consequences of CRs, or continuing resolutions, when we have been unable to reach budget deals that would provide a long-term vision in the budgeting process. CRs eliminate the long view, and they put the country on short-term budget appropriations. Short-term budgeting is far more expensive than long-term budgeting and planning, and most of our military expenditures are cheaper when we're able to take the long view over a longer window of time. For example, our most recent continuing resolution could have cost our military about $1.2 billion a month, and we've had a few dozen CRs or short-term funding resulting in very inefficient use of taxpayer dollars over the last decade or more. Many of our congressional leaders are failing civics because they are failing to understand the implications of short-term thinking.

Though I failed four subjects in ninth grade, I knew even then that my teachers were not at fault. Their performance was not in question. The fact remained that I liked to talk in class. It just came naturally to me. My teachers could give me as direct a warning as possible, but their words did not really affect me. One of my favorite teachers, Mrs. Lynch, told me that my clowning around during English would not affect her ability to teach the class, but it would certainly affect my ability to pass the class. My effort was unsatisfactory, and multiple report cards reflected my teachers' strong perspectives. My effort did not match my ability—*period*. I could do the work, but I chose not to. It hardly mattered that their comments said I was a joy to have in class. A joyful countenance doesn't earn a diploma—the student must do the work.

Unfortunately, during my freshman year, my appetite for getting laughs and playing the role of the jock meant that my grades were lower than the number of push-ups I could do. When I basically failed my freshman year of high school, I found my rock bottom. To advance, I had to take summer school classes. My mom could not afford the classes, and even if she could have, she wouldn't have paid for them. I was going to pay for summer school or repeat ninth grade. Neither option was very appealing, but thankfully, I ended up earning enough money to pay for the classes.

After earning a chance to become a sophomore, I got a job working at the movie theater. There I made some lifelong friends, including two who would forever change my life. The amazing thing was that I had been hired at the movie theater by sheer chance. My friends Roger Yongue and Lewis Atkins were working there, and one day as they were cleaning windows at the front of the theater, they overheard the manager say they needed to hire someone right away. A couple of employees had quit, and they were very short-staffed. As that conversation was happening, I came walking through the mall and past the movie theater. Roger pointed at me and said to his manager, "Hey, Tim is a great guy, I'm sure he would be perfect!" I got hired on the spot. How's that for providence?!

Forty-plus years later, the names of Roger Yongue, Danny Tolentino, and a host of others still bring a smile to my face. Northwoods Mall was basically like a city, where we had a multiethnic group of young folks hanging out and growing up together. It was the summer when we would have the most fun, and the fall when we would memorize lines from the movies we played for too long with far too few people watching them. One of our friends, Danny

Durant, picked up the nickname "Sweet Pea" from *An Officer and a Gentleman*, starring Richard Gere.

We played that movie for twenty-plus weeks! I will always remember Louis Gossett Jr. saying to Gere, "What's the matter with you, Sweet Pea?" as he went through training to become an officer. This was also the time when Sylvester Stallone would carve his name in Hollywood history with the Rocky movies. We worked *Rocky III,* and I still remember the crowds winding around the corners in the mall.

What an absolute blast we had, serving popcorn and sodas while hundreds of people descended on the single-screen theater for the blockbuster summer hits. We worked sunup to sundown. Seventy-hour workweeks were the norm for the start of the summer movie season. I loved it, and there was no better time to be at work than when it was busy.

While I was initially thrilled with the opportunity to make some money and help my mom pay bills around the house, I ended up being forever thankful to have good friends and lots of fun during the summertime. Life was simple, and our resources were scarce. We had our group of friends, but none closer to me than Roger. I respected and appreciated him and his family. His dad was a good, hardworking man who seemed thoroughly dedicated to his family, and his mom was a rock that all of us would and could lean on. You will hear his name throughout the rest of this book, as we are still best friends to this very day.

A NETWORK OF OPPORTUNITIES

I'm a big proponent of the idea that there are no self-made people. There is a special place for teachers and professionals who, instead of telling you how hard it will be, tell you how strong you will become. Instead of reminding you of your disadvantages, they help you see your natural gifts and skills, also known as your natural advantages.

Another person who did this for me was not a teacher in my life, at least not in the professional sense. No, he was an entrepreneur who ran a Chick-fil-A. His name is John Moniz, and he truly changed my life.

John would bring his kids to work sometimes, and they would hang out at the movie theater while he was running his restaurant at the mall. After seeing me buy french fries at Chick-fil-A a few times, John came down to the movie theater to see just who it was his children were hanging out with. He came to the theater, and he won me over when he slid a Chick-fil-A sandwich across the table. French fries have always been the fastest way to my heart, and he coupled it with a sandwich I couldn't afford. Right then, I was all ears for whatever he might say next. Over the next few minutes, John asked me about my life and my goals, and it really felt like he was trying to get to know me.

From that moment on, John taught me many lessons. He taught me that having a job was a good thing, but creating jobs for others would be a great thing. He taught me that taking a paycheck home was awesome, but that creating profits would be fantastic. He introduced me to the motivational teachings of Zig Ziglar, who attended the University of South Carolina, on audio-cassette tapes. Through the magic of technology, I still listen to them, now as audiobooks. From then on, John became my mentor.

John encouraged my football dreams, but he also encouraged me to think on a grander scale. Even if I made it to the NFL, John showed me that I would still need a plan for my future. Back then, players were not compensated nearly as well as they are now, and life would not stop at thirty-five years old or whenever I retired. If I was lucky enough to make good money, I would still need to know what to do with it. Even now we see this issue as so many professional athletes go bankrupt after the checks stop coming, no matter how many millions they made. These lessons from John were the keys to my financial literacy, and they became a foundational pillar of my ideology.

I remember John pulling into the mall parking lot in this brand-new, shiny and long, white Lincoln Continental. That was the definition of a luxurious car back in those days, and it caught everyone's attention. But he did not drive it because he was rich and could afford it. Rather, he won it from Chick-fil-A, due to his store's outstanding performance. Years later, when I visited the Chick-fil-A headquarters in Atlanta, I saw a picture hanging on the wall, a photo of John shaking hands with Chick-fil-A founder S. Truett Cathy—in front of that very same Lincoln Continental. That's the kind of story I wanted to emulate.

My big-time football dreams came to an end after my car flipped across Interstate 26. I had broken my ankle, and I missed about half of my senior season. Safe to say, it was a great thing that I had gotten my academics on track. I ended up earning a partial football scholarship to Presbyterian College, a small school in Clinton, South Carolina. But I knew that football was no longer my path forward.

My journey through middle and high school ended up teaching me an important lesson, and one that I share during commencement speeches I give today. That lesson is this: failure is not fatal unless you quit. At any point in this process, I could have thrown my hands up, and I could have ended up dead or in jail, like too many kids from my neighborhood. Thankfully, my mom and John Moniz ensured that wouldn't happen.

John started teaching me what I now recognize as some of the foundations of conservative ideology. Back then, it just made sense as I began to get my life back on track.

I needed to learn to buckle down and get the work done. A good education at Stall High School wasn't simply about the academics; it was about life skills as well. My teachers required that I learn to be a thinker. We learned *how* to think, not *what* to think. Sure, it's important to challenge the status quo, and my teachers encouraged us to push back. But facts had to be our lead card, not our feelings. That powerful lesson seems to be missing today, as I encounter so many people who base their strongest decisions on their emotions or headline news—not the facts of the actual events. My teachers made sure that I was a good thinker.

I could go on for many paragraphs and pages about these teachers who changed my life. Mrs. Lynch, Ms. Cabe, Mrs. Greenburg, and Mrs. Warden—these powerful women embraced me when I was down, looked beyond my performance, and demanded better from me. They knew I had more in me, and they wanted me to do better. Each one disciplined me for my lack of concentration and focus, but they also encouraged my warm and friendly personality. These educators did not believe in lowering their standards, but rather it was their goal to raise my expectations of myself. This is the language of transformation in the lives of students, as some of us do our best work as a result of second chances.

SECOND CHANCES

We need some of that attitude in our nation right now, where too often we look for the easy way out instead of making uncomfortable choices. America became the greatest nation on earth because we took on the challenges no one else would and we made hard choices. We did not shirk our duty. Through the will and spirit of the American people, we succeeded.

Sometimes it seems we don't recognize that we must earn the title of being the best. It won't just be given to us. It's easier, for example, to pass continuing resolutions to fund the government, but the country would be better served by setting long-term budget priorities. As always, the temptation to take the easy path can seem irresistible.

Advanced technology has given us inviting temptations to make everything easier in all aspects of our lives. So, we go with the flow and avoid the tough challenges of using our brains to win successes. But such easy successes are won without the bitter taste of small failures along the way—small failures that are great teaching tools. In fact, we have become afraid to fail, and that alone is a problem.

Take, as an example, Walt Disney as a young reporter. Today, the Walt Disney kingdom is undeniable. His impact on the lives of millions and millions of youngsters is etched into our memory in American history books and so much of our everyday life. But at the beginning of his career, the story was quite different. The story of Walt Disney was a story of failure. He was fired from his first job because he lacked creativity. Walt Disney!

But in America, people get a second chance. And with that second chance, places like Disney World and Disneyland continue to inspire the creativity of millions of people because they understand how to inspire and motivate. Disney is a company driven by imagination and creativity, a company founded by someone who was once fired for lacking those skills.

America is the land of second chances, and I've often referred to America as the land of redemption. I have seen this firsthand, because of the second chances that I believe my family and community gave to me.

"My faith is the essence of my existence . . . It is, in its essence, a love story, about God's love for humanity, and the lengths that he is willing to go and the sacrifices that he made for us to spend all eternity with him."

—FROM A WASHINGTON EXAMINER *INTERVIEW WITH RUDY TAKALA, APRIL 25, 2016*

CHAPTER 6

A LIGHT IN CLINTON, SOUTH CAROLINA

"ABSOLUTELY NOT!!!!!!!!" These two words changed the course of my church's history.

Seacoast Church is a nondenominational church in Mount Pleasant, South Carolina, and it has exploded in growth over the last couple of decades. Back in 1999, we were a much smaller church, and our membership was growing exponentially. We were looking to expand our facility in order to accommodate the growth, so we approached the town of Mount Pleasant with some possible ways to go about it.

They didn't say, "Let's consider all the alternatives."

They didn't say, "We're not sure this is the best option."

And they didn't even quietly decline. They said, "Absolutely not." And they followed their final word with many exclamation points.

This may not sound shocking to everyone, but to a small bedroom community in the suburbs of Charleston, often called "The Holy City" with its four hundred steepled churches, we were shocked to see the town of Mount Pleasant respond so adamantly. It was a decision with consequences that would reverberate for the next two decades.

81

You see, the town of Mount Pleasant saw our church as a nuisance. We were growing faster than they had anticipated, and they did not want any traffic congestion that a growing church would cause—even for just a few hours a week on Sunday mornings and Wednesday evenings.

I could not believe my ears. At the time, I was the vice chairman of the Charleston County Council, and when I heard such words of defiance, I decided to fight fire with fire. My response was, "Let's just beat them all."

I wasn't calling for a violent protest, but I wanted to take the city fathers out of office and beat them with the influence of voters. The answer seemed crystal clear! Let's just beat them at the ballot box and this delay will not deny us! Let's beat all the members of the town council, replace them all, and build our church.

Pastor Greg Surratt is the founder of the church, and he had a different perspective—which, honestly, I didn't appreciate at the time. He said, "Let's pray about it."

Now, I will concede that today, the words "Let's pray about it" are commonplace in my vocabulary. I say that often. It means a lot when I choose to pray about it. It's not inaction. Rather, I know it's the greatest action I can take, and I have learned this in part because of the amazing experience we encountered with Mount Pleasant. Instead of taking a political solution to the town council, my pastor encouraged me and my strong will to be patient and see what God might do. I wanted a political remedy and a beatdown at the ballot box. But instead, he invited me and the entire church into seventeen days of praying and fasting.

For those of you who may be unfamiliar—as I was—with the concept of fasting, let's talk about that for a moment. Fasting is when you intentionally separate yourself from something you enjoy. You gather the energy you would have once given to that thing you enjoyed, and you channel that time and energy to discern God's will in your life, community, or church. Pastor Greg invited us to a seventeen-day fast that would end before Thanksgiving. (Even our pastor knew it was a tall order to ask us not to break our fast but to give thanks!) He encouraged us to fast from one thing of value in our own lives: fast food, watching TV, listening to the radio in the car, certain forms of entertainment—any habit that could easily distract us from hearing wisdom that we desperately needed. We spent more than two weeks fasting and praying about what to do, and at the end of the seventeen-day fast, we had our new direction.

My pastor announced his decision: to acquiesce. He chose to submit to the authority of the town. He decided to honor the town, and he would do this by serving God in any way the Lord saw fit. This was a real disappointment to me, and those are the gentlest words I can use. I was deeply troubled by this choice.

I was on the church's board of trustees at the time, and we began discussing how to overcome this great challenge we faced. We thought about moving out of the town, but my pastor anchored himself in the truth that our church was located where the Lord wanted us to be, and the only question was how to grow when you are stuck between a rock and a hard place.

So, we started investigating the idea of multiple locations. We opened a satellite location where we could have live praise and worship with a simulcast of the sermon, and this started in a shopping center we had rented around the corner. We had already strategized for the young professionals to meet in this location, and this would free up space for other activities in the primary church. With a little tweaking, we decided to turn that location into our first satellite location.

Pastor Greg wisely decided that we would not figure this out on our own, and he invited consultants who had expertise with multiple locations of a local restaurant chain: Sticky Fingers. We asked them to teach us how to run multiple locations from one main branch, and our conversation unfolded over numerous meetings, several hours each. We wanted to minimize our mistakes and maximize our opportunities, and we wanted to utilize a successful formula we could weave into the areas of faith and church growth. Out of that discussion with Sticky Fingers, and out of the "Absolutely Not!!!!" from Mount Pleasant, we arrived at a giant yes: our decision to become a multisite church.

As Pastor Greg discovered that resources for church planting were little to none, he partnered with his good friend Billy Hornsby, a Cajun from Louisiana, to launch a church planting organization called the Association of Related Churches, or the ARC. The goal was to provide seed funding, management expertise, and other necessary resources that new churches need to get started, open their doors, and to succeed. ARC began to provide help and opportunities to grow young churches and expand the impact on the faith community as well as the unchurched community.

We have had tremendous success over the last twenty years because of the ARC. Today, in 2020, we have more than 900 churches, with an average weekly attendance of over 500,000 people, including the second-largest church in the nation, located in Birmingham, Alabama. Greg's vision, his strong desire to submit himself to the authority of the town of Mount Pleasant, turned out to be one of the most remarkable events in our church's history. Today, hundreds of churches have modeled their multiple locations after Seacoast's multisite model. Not only were we able to grow the size of our own church through multiple locations, but we have also been blessed to see hundreds of churches across the nation do the exact same thing. Seacoast became the primary resource for church leaders to learn how to expand into multisite churches. This success can be traced back to a major obstacle that turned into a great opportunity.

Too often, we think we know exactly what to do because it's so obvious. I learned that it's conceivable that there's a better plan at work. Always do what you can do. If you can't change the minds, learn to ride the waves as you make them.

Incidentally, in 2019, we opened the building we had attempted to build decades ago in Mount Pleasant. God is good.

MY FAITH JOURNEY

When I showed up at Presbyterian College (PC) in 1983, I felt like a fish out of water. I had moved away from everything familiar in Charleston, and I was in a smaller town in Clinton, the heart of South Carolina's upstate. I was three hours from home, but I might as well have been on Mars. This small town was a complete and total culture shock. I missed my mom, my friends, and my home.

On top of that, PC was a newly integrated college, and the first African-American student had enrolled just a little more than a decade before me. The racial divisions in the town were obvious. Like many small towns in the South, at the center of town was a memorial to soldiers who lost their lives in the Civil War. I had experienced racism in Charleston, but there I knew what to expect and where to avoid those sorts of issues. Now that I was dropped into a rural town of eight thousand with only a few dozen or so African-Americans in the student body of about twelve hundred, I had to navigate those new minefields while I was learning how to live on my own. I had grown up in a place friendlier to minorities, so it was a strange experience to consistently hear open aggression from others. I heard the N-word many times off and on campus, and if it were not for my teammates like Del Barksdale and Greg Kinsey, I'm not sure I would have made it a month. It's no surprise I didn't go off campus much, as the pain and loneliness from being away from home was compounded by a sense of alienation from so many others.

Far more upsetting than any racial division, however, was the loss of my sense of self.

The transition—from the top of the food chain in high school down to the first rung on the ladder in college—was eye opening. Football and student government had given me lots of friends and instant popularity in high school, but no one cared about that at PC. My aunt has always reminded me that when I was a senior in high school, my ego was so big that they had to turn me sideways to get my big head into the building. I wouldn't entirely agree with that, but she thought she had a better perspective on who I was. I had a lot of potential and talent. But now I was a high school standout who was starting all over again. I had lost my way. I had lost my secret sauce. I went to football practices, but they did not mean as much to me anymore. Everything felt empty.

My goal had always been to play professional football, and I had come to PC on a partial football scholarship. But the car accident just before my senior year permanently changed my trajectory. I was no longer as focused on football as I was simply thankful to be alive, walking and talking, and able to enjoy my life. That's when I began to understand that there must be more to life than simply the things that had been important to me. Regarding football, I think "the new car smell" had faded a little, and the sheen had worn off a bit.

When I reflect on that season of my life, there were so many moving parts: the loss of my focus on football, being away from home, a rigorous academic schedule, and most important, my search for meaning. It was a perfect formula to launch me into a place of soul-searching. Things changed for me, and I had not yet figured out my future path. I still felt like the Lord had a plan for my life, but I couldn't figure out what it was.

In truth, my faith journey started back at the movie theater. We were working overtime one night when I found myself asking Roger a question about happiness. He was always so cheerful, and to be honest (and blunt), I could not understand why. He lived in a trailer and he drove a car that was twenty years old. In fact, his life matched up pretty closely with mine, as we lived in an apartment complex next to the trailer park, and we drove a Gremlin. As I've already mentioned, the Gremlin was a far cry from a Cadillac!

So, that summer, as we were pouring Coca-Cola behind the concession stand, Roger gave me the simplest of answers. It was nearly impossible for me to understand. I asked him, "Why are you so happy, Roger?"

His response was, "Because Jesus Christ is the Lord of my life!"

I was quick with my retort. "That's it?"

I was almost frustrated by the simplicity of his answer. He responded just as quickly, "Yes."

I thought, *But you live in a trailer, work your butt off all the time, and your answer to a question of happiness and bliss was simply Jesus Christ is Lord of your life?* It was an insufficient answer, and I wanted more information. Why is he the Lord of your life? And how does that make you so happy? I needed to know. I did not understand the power of simple commitments. A big lesson with a new perspective was coming my way.

A BETTER PLAN

During my personal turmoil as a freshman in college, I had the fortune of having a fantastic captain of the football team, John "J.R." Rickenbaucher. He became the key to helping me adjust to the demands of being an athlete at a college where academics were the number one priority. It was a lot to manage!

I laugh now thinking about the fact that football practice was late on Mondays because we all had to attend lab first. I'm not saying it is not the same at other universities, but I have been on quite a few campuses at this point in my life, and PC certainly seemed to take academics more seriously than many others.

Coach Rickenbaucher was involved in the Fellowship of Christian Athletes (FCA), which turned out to be a gigantic influence in my life. As much as I loved football, I could feel it becoming less of a focus as I attended other important things, like Bible study and FCA meetings. As we talked about the goodness of God in the land of the living, I realized he would provide me with an unshakable foundation that football never could. In the same way that John Moniz had begun teaching me about conservative business principles, J.R. and the FCA were now truly showing me the life-changing possibilities of accepting Jesus Christ as my Savior.

Around September 22, 1983, when I walked out of my dorm room and into a meeting for Fellowship of Christian Athletes, I did not know that I would enter that meeting as a questioning wanderer and leave as an entirely new creation in Christ. It was a run-of-the-mill evening at the school, and I found myself in a small room seated in a small circle to discuss the Bible. When J.R. gave an altar call, something in my heart answered. In a room full of fifteen or twenty people, I felt like I was the only one. It was like when the stage goes dark and the spotlight shines on the star of the show. In that moment, the Lord was listening to my prayer, as if I were the only one on the earth.

Many people have heard me quote the Scripture that says, "People without a vision perish," but my vision was being adjusted. In many ways, I was humbled enough to embrace a better plan. I did lose a lot of the scholarships due to the car accident, but by losing, I was actually winning. The loss of scholarships led me to find a better plan, a better focus, a bigger field, a bigger stage. And not just for a few years of professional football, but for a life of service. That's the greatest lesson I learned at Presbyterian College.

Today I understand the simple truth that one must be born again to gain eternal life. However, when I was younger, the concept of being "born again" was foreign to me. Even after becoming an adult, I struggled with this notion. Nicodemus asked that same question with confusion in John 3 when he said, "Can I enter the birth canal again?" Nicodemus was puzzled, too! However, it wasn't the complications that caused me pause. It was the effortlessness of rebirth that puzzled me. We went to church every Sunday anyway, so the thought of needing a jolt to recharge my faith was not on my radar. As a religious kid, I could not imagine a system that measured my life not by my actions, but rather by a grace given by faith alone.

In college, Jesus became everything to me. I even bought a sweatshirt that said, "Football is my game, and Jesus is my life." What a shift, right? But I have to say, upon my conversion, I became almost a little over the top with my faith. I didn't want anyone around me to focus on anything other than the Gospel, Christianity, and growing their faith. I became a fairly religious person, and I don't say that as a compliment to myself, but as a negative observation. Ultimately, the religious spirit condemns instead of convicting, thus bringing us closer to the Lord. That religious judgment isn't good for the soul, and it certainly isn't good for salvation. It took me a long time to learn that lesson, to set aside that perspective. Even now, I feel I probably should apologize to my roommate for thinking that he should be reading his Bible all the time. I was simply being judgmental.

Because of my own ego as a new Christian, I had placed so much emphasis on a rules-based system that I had missed the love story that is faith. To understand a love story, you must first understand that love is not simply an emotion. It's a commandment. The Gospel is very clear: "If you love me, you will keep my commandments." That does not mean that we will perfectly do everything he wants us to do, or that we will feel everything he wants us to feel. But it means that if I love the Lord, I will follow the word of the Lord.

FAITH OF OUR FOREFATHERS

An intern once asked me whether I should leave my faith at home when it comes to my decisions on Capitol Hill. She was concerned that my faith would make it harder for me to support legislation she thought was important to people, especially issues around life. She asked how I keep my faith from being intermingled with my politics, and my response to her was simple: I don't.

There's no doubt that my faith informs me in every facet of my life. I wanted her to understand that we don't leave our core values at home when we serve in public office.

I think the essence of who you are should be reflected in your public service. None of us should be responsible to eliminate our faith in order to serve the nation. Rather, it is because of my faith that I want to serve the nation in such a way that even when you disagree with me, you still have the right to be heard and to proclaim what you believe to be true.

Each of us brings a set of values to everything we do. The origins of those values are important. However, in America we don't separate our values from our public service. My Democratic friends have spoken clearly on their faith informing their decisions. Former vice president Joe Biden said that his Catholic faith informs him on every decision. I shared with this young lady that it is impossible to separate our faith from our values, and we should never hope to.

In America, we welcome everyone from everywhere, no matter their faith—or the lack of it. What we never do, and must not do, is ask anyone to leave it at home. The Constitution was designed to protect our faith from the government, not the government from our faith. As I was answering her, I stood there thinking to myself about the importance of my daily rituals: reading a section from the book of Proverbs every day, followed by good uplifting music and a Bible study. Without this daily regimen, I would be less prepared to deal with the challenges and the negativity of working in a swamp. I am reminded of a quote by Abraham Lincoln: "I have been driven many times upon my knees by the overwhelming conviction that I had nowhere else to go."

I am sure that today more and more people believe our faith should not influence our public life; however, that is a grave mistake. It again was Abraham Lincoln who reminded us that we should have charity toward all and malice toward none, as we held this union together in the aftermath of the Civil War. His thoughts were faith filled, and he quoted from the Bible in his second inaugural address.

I am not afraid of a debate on the ideas regarding what is best for our future. What concerns me is that we've entered into a stage where the civility that is necessary for strong, healthy discourse is seeping out of our society. The fastest way to plug the hole is to find things we have in common, things that allow us to continue the conversation about the future and less about the past.

A STORY OF REDEMPTION

The story of salvation to me is a story of redemption. I was lost, and I have been found. I was blind, and I can now see. Our nation is going through that, although from an inverted perspective. We have been found, but we are losing ourselves as faith begins to lose its prominence in society. Once we could see, and our vision is growing dark and dim without that compass. It was John Adams who said, "America cannot survive this experiment in self-governance unless we are both a moral and a religious people."

He said that not because he was gung-ho on religion, but because he understood that without some rules and boundaries that are eternal, absolute, and objective, we don't stand a chance in this experiment of self-governance that gives us the ability to give to ourselves more than we can afford to keep. There is a higher source of our right and wrongs. We don't decide that for ourselves; that is called relativism.

What we forget today in America is the importance of that foundation as a nation. Our foundation is the light. It's part of what makes us the city on a hill. Our foundation of faith is part of why we are the most philanthropic nation on earth. It's one of the reasons why we have produced the best outcomes economically, not only for our own people, but for the world. It's one of the reasons why we have decided to participate in places of conflict, where we believe it is part of our mission. Am I my brother's keeper? The answer is yes.

Now, we can't define that as the whole world all the time, because we don't have the resources and people power to do that all the time. But there is no doubt that who we are as a nation requires us to do things that other nations—according to their founding documents—are not tasked with doing. It's one of the reasons we have lifted ourselves to become the most prosperous, powerful, amazing country on earth.

If we had a mission statement in America, it would include Psalm 122:6: Pray for the peace of Jerusalem, and those who do will prosper. The role that faith has played in our nation is so significant that it set the stage for who we have been for 240 years. We have done it so imperfectly that it only reinforces the necessity of a Savior, of something outside of ourselves that must validate good versus bad. In a relative world, in a relative nation, we lose most of our significance. Without an objective standard based on absolute truth, our legal system frays so much so that in the heart of our land, people don't know what we stand for.

It is the loss of that clear focus that has led us to have one of the higher suicide rates in the world. We live in the most prosperous land on earth, and yet so many take their own lives because they have lost hope. And certainly, we could talk about the abortion rate, the number of people that we've lost, 60-million-plus Americans who will never touch our soil. Without a mission and a clear vision, the light loses some of its meaning.

Without that steadfast approach to pursuing something more than yourselves, the salt is no longer salty. Society today is so caught up in me, myself, and I. What do I want? Deserve? Need? That's not part of the American fabric. "Ask not what your country can do for you, but what you can do for your country." That comes from a Judeo-Christian foundation that holds the golden rule, Matthew 7: 12, "Do unto others as you would have them do unto you," and Galatians 6:7, "It is better to give than to receive." These truths are woven into the fabric of our nation.

I have experienced the good Lord taking lemons and making lemonade, and after attending Bible study for a while, I experienced the sweetest lemonade of all. On the night I gave my life to Jesus, he changed my perspective forever. This conversion is important to every facet of my life. As I think through my faith, I must concede that every good thing I do in my life comes back to that experience at Presbyterian College. There is no question that this conversion made Jesus not just my Savior, but my Lord.

The difference is incredibly important from my perspective. When people asked Jesus, "What is the most important commandment in the law?" Jesus answered with two: Love the

Lord your God with all your heart, soul, and mind. This is the first and most important commandment. And the second most important commandment is similar. And it is, "Love others as much as you love yourself" (Matthew 22:36–39 CEV). God has called us to love him with everything we are, but the second most important calling is how we treat each other. I learned the lessons of Matthew 7: 12—"Do unto others as you would have them do unto you"—during that time at PC. I learned it from two different sources: the people who treated me differently for whatever reason, maybe because I was a jock, or an African-American, or because I was from Charleston and not from another part of the state. Whatever their reason, I walked away with an understanding and an appreciation for what not to do when trying to treat others as I'd like to be treated.

Second, I learned how to treat others the way I do want to be treated. My friends at P.C. introduced me not only to eternal life, but they also taught me a lot about friendships. Friendships that are bonded together through pressure, pain, and practice—football practice, that is. Those lessons stay with me today.

As I find myself immersed in the nation's capital, at times in a Bible study or a prayer breakfast, I can look across the room and see a lot of people who are not like me. I see folks from different parts of the country; people of different races, ethnicities, genders, backgrounds; some who may be more skeptical in their faith, others who are thriving in their faith. I've been able to leverage my time at Presbyterian College to serve the nation.

We are trying to test the ends of those definitions right now, but I think we can find our way back. As a man who was once lost but now found, once blind but now sees, I know how it is to be in the wilderness. My hope is that we will spend enough time reexamining the foundation of this nation, flaws and all, in order to realize the greatness of this nation. To me, that's the story of salvation and redemption.

MY INSPIRATION

What I found at Presbyterian College was neither a new secret sauce nor a new motivation. I found inspiration. I was inspired by a truth that transcends all time, and that truth was the sacrifice of one person for all of humanity. I arrived as a kid who was bright, funny, and a little self-absorbed. I found and recognized a transformation that altered my mission into serving others, not myself.

I thank God for the seeds that were sown in my junior and senior year of high school. I must give credit to Roger Yongue, my best friend, for a persistent, consistent, optimistic, jovial response to an age-old question, "Why are you so happy?" It's been asked a billion times by more than a billion people. He gave a very simple answer, with the power of eternity. Jesus Christ is the only way. He is the way, the truth, and the light. With him, you never perish, and that alone is reason enough to be happy. Not your circumstances, your situations, or your resources. It's not who you're with or who you know. The answer is simply one man who died on a Friday and rose on a Sunday to be the King of kings and the Lord of lords.

THE OPPORTUNITY FOR AMERICA

I now know that faith is woven into the DNA of our country. We may not all believe the same, but we share a common thread through our history. Our faith helped the enslaved persevere through the original sin of our country, and our faith helped us to forgive after the Mother Emanuel church shooting. Our country's future and its past has hung on our freedom to live and to worship as we choose. Frederick Douglass fought for freedom because of our foundation's focus on inalienable rights. Our founders embraced a unique concept, that all men are created equally, even if imperfectly. The opportunity for America in a pluralist society is to hold on to the truths that are self-evident, the truth that all men and women are created equal, and inherent in our creation are inalienable rights that include life, liberty, and the pursuit of happiness. To live freely will require us to protect the religious liberties that are under attack today throughout our great country.

We see anti-Semitism on the rise on college campuses across the country. Members of Congress trafficking in age-old Jewish tropes to support their anti-Israel agenda. Christian colleges are under attack. Even the second lady of the United States came under fire for announcing she would teach art at a Christian school in Virginia. Freedom of religion was written into the Constitution for a reason, and there is no doubt that our nation's founders, despite their flaws, were men of faith.

Without a faith journey, I would not care more for my fellow countrymen than I do for myself. Without my faith, I would not focus on preserving the country passed onto me that includes your freedom to disagree and my responsibility to die for your right to do so, as more than a million Americans have done for our freedoms.

America's greatness is inextricably linked to our goodness. We may test it at our own peril if we must, but the outcome is not in question. French diplomat Alexis de Tocqueville foreshadowed this doom when he said that America will cease to be great when America ceases to be good. The goodness of America was not found in our institutions of government or education or commerce; it was our churches that were bursting with the fire of conviction and worship. These are what caught the French diplomat by surprise.

It's the same fire that saved my state from a racist gunman who walked into a black church and executed nine believers in order to start a race riot. They responded with love for their enemy, and this approach both saved and changed my state and this nation. The world watched and wondered what was different in South Carolina. It is this same faith that stands as the last and most powerful hope our country has to shape a world in search of meaning without God.

Of course, I did not know all that as a college student. I just knew that something in me called me to the Lord during my freshman year at Presbyterian. Oddly enough, while you might think that was an immediately gratifying feeling, it was somewhat different for me. I truly loved football, and then I knew that the plan for my life did not include it. For a while, I tearfully considered quitting both football and college so that I could pursue leadership and Christian growth above all else.

I left Presbyterian College after my freshman year; I chose to continue with college, but to transfer to a different one. I attended the institution that was then called the Baptist College (now Charleston Southern University) to earn my degree. I left Clinton, South Carolina, but it has held a sacred space in my heart. What I found in Clinton gave me a light to chase, a purpose to fulfill. I have been back to Clinton a few times since then, and I have found the people so welcoming and kind. One of my teammates, Stacy Drakeford, has even become the first African-American director of public safety for Clinton. This is proof: just as I have grown, so has Clinton. Perhaps I just needed the wisdom that comes with age and the ability to better understand the world around me.

It's amazing to realize that what once seemed like the only way forward was in fact a stepping-stone to a higher purpose—a purpose I could not see until football had been removed. I thought sports would be the only way to fulfill my dream and give my mom the safety and security she deserved. After I left PC, I realized that my mentor John Moniz had been sowing the seeds for many years, preparing me for the discovery of my true purpose.

THE DEATH OF MY FRIEND

In a devastating turn of events after I returned home to North Charleston, John died of a coronary embolism at just thirty-eight years old. John had been experiencing some pain and discomfort in his chest, and he finally decided to go see a doctor. The initial diagnosis was inaccurate, and the doctors missed the chance to save his life. My friend went to sleep, jolted awake a few minutes later, and had a cardiac event that was so extraordinarily strong that it literally knocked him off the bed and into the wall behind him as his beautiful wife, Janice, sat there beside him.

At the age of thirty-eight, he was gone. My mentor who had invested so very much into me had died. I was only fifteen years old when we met, but his impact on my life will live on. He had invested four years of his life in me, and he helped me discover that my true purpose was not football, but influence. I am reminded of Romans 8:28, which says that all things work together for good for those who love God and are called according to his purpose. I do not believe that God causes bad things to happen—like my dad leaving, my car wreck, or John suddenly dying. Instead, I believe that he leverages these terrible things for our own good.

It's amazing how the last four years of John's life actually became the first four years of my new life. The pain of John's loss reverberated in my heart and soul, because he had done so much with absolutely no reason to be involved. What was the payoff for him? He only gave and gave and gave, and he did not live long enough to receive the payback of his vision. I was truly blessed to have the opportunity to know John during the prime of his life. He inspired me with what he said *and* the way he lived.

John was a man with a generous spirit, and his entire family reflected that. His wife , Janice, was, in many ways, like a second mom to me during those times. Often on Mother's Day, I brought her roses and thanked her for including me in so many activities with their family. Janice was a kind person, and always encouraging. We had many conversations about dating, my future, and the prospects of changing the world. John and Janice were a couple with a singular focus, and that was really incredible for me to watch, especially since I had been raised in a single-parent household. Janice's strength and perseverance has been demonstrated in a remarkable way, as she has had to carry on as a widow, as a mother of three, and as the owner of a franchise.

I am friends with the Moniz family to this day. I got to spend a lot of time with their three children, Lauren, Brian, and Phillip. Lauren was usually at the store rather than at the video arcade with us boys, so I had the privilege of trying to do for John's sons what John had done for me. One of the tragic consequences of John's passing was the truly severe effect it would have on his family, especially his boys. Brian was young when his dad died, so I have tried to share my own stories of his dad with him, so that he has a complete picture of how amazing his dad truly was. As anyone would expect, Brian has struggled with the loss of his father for years.

I aimed to befriend Brian in the same ways that his father befriended me. Brian attended the Citadel, a military college in South Carolina, for just a year or two before he decided to take a different route. I remember sitting with Brian outside the mall, asking him if the Citadel, where his father attended college, was where he wanted to be. I sensed that he chose the school more to honor his father, and less because it was a good fit for him. Brian is a very smart guy, and he discovered quickly that it might indeed be better for him to choose a different path. Of course, he wanted to follow in the footsteps of his father's success at the highest level of an organization, and certainly Brian did just that. He operated a successful Chick-fil-A of his own for several years.

I was in Brian's wedding, and I spoke at his graduation from the South Carolina police academy in 2013. Brian and Philip are both sheriff's deputies now, and Brian is happier than he's ever been as a Charleston County sheriff's deputy. To know these men is to understand the dedication and loyalty that their father's life inspired in them. One of the obvious lessons that both Brian and Phillip learned from their father was a lesson of service. Law enforcement has never been more difficult, and these two young men are fully equipped and prepared. In fact, they were prepared before they became officers, prepared before they ever became fathers, and prepared before they ever became husbands. They were prepared by a role model and a father who didn't just teach the lessons of life—he lived them. He's one of the reasons why I say leadership is caught, not necessarily taught. In the Moniz household, John modeled these values for his sons, and they caught them with their hearts, souls, and minds.

In January 2010, our local newspaper, the *Charleston Post and Courier*, featured a story on National Mentorship Month, and they shared a short snippet of my journey with John as the lead segment in their story. It brought back so many glorious memories of the good times and his powerful impact.

Janice called the day the story about John and me ran, and I still remember where I was when I took her call—I was pulling into a parking garage in downtown Charleston. We laughed and cried together, enjoying and remembering all that John had done in such a short life. Less than four decades aren't very long on this earth, and it's even shorter when you're doing so much amazing work of loving people and loving life. John welcomed me, a random kid from North Charleston, into his family. He changed my life forever. That's not something you find every day.

The magnitude of his passing illuminates why I opened a notebook on the night before John's funeral, when I penned my life's mission statement: "Before I die, I will positively affect the lives of a billion people with a message of hope, which comes from my faith in Jesus Christ, and opportunity, through financial literacy and independence." I chose to honor John's life and memory by making his mission part of my own, and I claim it as my mission even today.

I try to speak to students every month, whether in person or by skype from my D.C. office, and when speaking to these wonderful youngsters, my mission statement renews itself greatly.

Last year I spoke at Newington Elementary School in Summerville and took questions from the students. The first question was from a cute eleven-year-old, fifth-grade girl named Adryen Rose. She asked me why I wanted to be a senator. Instantly my life's mission surfaced as I answered her question. Decades later, John's light still shines.

As a nation, we must remember our light, what brings us together, and how we can positively affect each other's lives. I have seen this every time I have traveled back to Clinton and Presbyterian College as an adult, as I have enjoyed connecting again with my teammates at our coach's funeral. I am drawn not only to the warm invitation I have received at football games or at a local school in the town, but I am also drawn to the spirit of the people. I can just feel the difference in the area. Communities are learning how to heal the rifts of the past and recognizing that division is not how America became great. We need to rebuild our faith in each other, and while we may not agree on the exact route, we all are together in the same direction: the future. Instead of constructing walls to separate ourselves, let's build bridges to stay connected.

"Asking people for money is giving them the opportunity to put their resources at the disposal of the Kingdom."

—HENRI NOUWEN

CHAPTER 7

THE BLAZING SPIRIT OF AN ENTREPRENEUR

A COUPLE OF YEARS AGO, a group of South Carolina lawmakers asked me to nominate a candidate for a federal judgeship. Now, I'm not opposed to unsolicited advice, but I could tell right away that these legislators—both Democrats and Republicans—did not have the best interests of my constituents in mind. They met in my office to present their "problem," which turned out to be a purely political matter. Put simply, they didn't approve of the front-runner an upcoming state judicial race, and their solution was to get me to appoint this person to a federal judgeship. If I would nominate that candidate to the federal bench, they figured, then he would not be in the running for the state judgeship. Basically, they had made a mess that they weren't willing to clean up, and they wanted to drop the problem into my lap.

I asked my friend Trey Gowdy to join us for the meeting. As a former federal prosecutor, he has unique insights into the judicial branch, and I always value his wisdom. Trey and I listened, and I was very clear with the legislators about my dismay. There were many problems with their plan.

First of all, the judge's beliefs were inconsistent with the philosophies I hold and support in concert with the Trump administration. In my view, the judge was not sufficiently conservative for the federal bench, but by nominating him it would make room for a more conservative-leaning state judge back in South Carolina. In other words, they wanted to make their problem go away by asking me to give this judge a promotion. I was not down for that.

Second, I knew that they had the ability to reach an amicable solution within the state, and they did not need my help to dig them out of the political quagmire where they found themselves. These lawmakers could easily win the votes in the general assembly and solve their own problems without putting me—and the federal court system—in a compromising position.

And third, I did not appreciate their efforts to kick their problem over to me. I do not like to be manipulated, and I have never responded positively when anyone tries to box me into a corner. I have learned what it looks like, and I can smell it from a mile away. You see, very few people lead with, "Here's what you should do." No, they are far more clever. Most people act like they're only here to give you friendly advice, but all the while they are trying to nudge you in their direction. The nuances are subtle, but learning to recognize the difference between the two is very important.

When you allow someone to tell you what to do, you can be sure they will keep coming back with stronger and more forceful demands. The best thing to do for yourself and your integrity is to say no from the start and keep moving in the right direction. Do not simply surrender when you feel you are at a disadvantage. If you feel like they are at their strongest, push out of that corner they've put you in. This keeps you on track, and it keeps your focus strong. Surrendering under pressure can become a lifestyle, and I do not recommend it.

When people demand that I do something, especially something that is obviously not in the best interests of my constituents, they are essentially ensuring that I will do the opposite. The South Carolina legislators were clearly unaware of this when they approached me with their plan. Spoiler alert: they did not get their nomination from me. Ultimately, they left not with what they wanted, but with what I had to give: my advice to never present to me a situation that doesn't benefit the nation and our state.

My mom can tell you that this is not a new pattern of mine; it has always been true. Whatever she told me specifically not to do became exactly the next thing I always did. If she said no, I said yes. And if she were sitting with you and me right now, she'd have a hundred examples. Even if her warning was valid, even if she was trying to protect me from physically harming myself, I resisted being told what to do.

That pattern continued throughout my youth. I messed with light sockets; I tried to jump over trash cans in a single bound on my bike; and I repeatedly tried to perform the magic trick of pushing a small piece of paper through my head, from my left ear through to my right ear. My brother tricked me into that last one, and I was determined to make it work—even when it once landed me in the hospital!

This tendency to go against the grain, to be independent, has stayed with me my entire life, and it's probably the reason I became an entrepreneur. I have always been determined to forge my own path by learning my own lessons and making my own decisions, and this is the way of the entrepreneur.

BUILDING BUSINESSES

In college, I got my start as an entrepreneur when I spent about four years working as a door-to-door salesman for Amway. I put John Moniz's lessons into action as I set out to succeed, developing my own network marketing team, and selling everything from food for your table to the vacuum cleaners to suck up the crumbs. I laugh now when I picture the scene. Imagine a young college student ringing doorbells until a nice grandmother opens the door. Her house is immaculate, the couch is covered in plastic, and even her trash cans seem clean. There I was, a twenty-year-old kid, trying to sell her a vacuum cleaner. She hardly wanted what I was selling.

But you can never underestimate what you learn in those situations. While the short-term success was some cash in my pocket, the long-term lessons were absolutely critical. I learned to listen to people's needs and concerns without simply waiting for my chance to talk. I got to speak with so many people from different backgrounds, and I got to listen to what makes them tick. I could never have gotten where I am without those lessons, and I learned to truly care about the people teaching me.

After I graduated from college, I got a job managing a men's clothing store. That's where I started to turn my dreams into concrete ideas. At that point, I was vacillating between two future plans: I might become a lawyer, or I might continue down this new sales path before me. I was praying a lot about that decision, when one day the answer appeared before my very eyes.

One Monday morning, a man walked into the store to buy a new suit. As any good salesman hopes to do, I also talked him into a new belt, some socks, and several other accessories. I didn't know it at the time, but he was the general sales manager for New York Life Insurance, and I had impressed him with my sales skills. It's hard to convince a salesman to purchase more than he planned to buy, but I had helped this man significantly expand his wardrobe. He told me I had a natural gift as a salesman, and I took his words to heart. That day, I claimed sales as my career.

I earned my license to sell life insurance, and I began working for New York Life. That company's training program is celebrated as one of the best in the industry, and my training manager, Ellen, taught me an important lesson for selling insurance and being effective in politics: know your audience. Ellen taught me it is not enough to know people's names, but it's essential to also learn what they believe and why they believe it.

One of my first tasks as a new agent was to make a list of five hundred people I know personally, and I found out very quickly that making a list of five hundred people was pretty tough. Looking back, I realize now that they were not training me to make the list, but rather how to multiply it. That skill came from the second step, which was the skill of earning referrals. When people are willing to put their name behind you, you have earned not only their trust, but the trust of their friends as well. I had learned yet another sales lesson that applies very well to politics.

New York Life also taught me about the importance of family planning, financial planning, and budgeting. I learned the importance of having a succession plan, and I communicated that value to folks when I asked them to consider what their families will do when they—or their income—are no longer around. Nothing lasts forever, and one thing we can be sure of is the end of our own lives. We do not know when, but we know it's coming. It's only wise to have a plan in place for the people we love most. Do you know what I discovered? That's not unique to families, and it's not just about insurance sales. It's a critical component to the health of our nation as a whole. We have got to keep thinking about how to equip the next generation for their chance to lead.

Ultimately, our ability to prepare this nation for the next generation requires us to have a succession planning model in mind. When your succession plan is crystal clear, your motivation and objectives are also clear. When a family spends everything they have, and they see their credit cards as extensions of their paychecks, it only leads to more debt. The same is true for our country: we are $22 trillion in debt and we continue to make plans for spending without making plans for saving. That is a formula for disaster for our nation. In Congress we have had many fruitless votes centered around reining in our national debt, and we will continue to have unsuccessful votes as long as our long-term thinking is faulty or—even worse—nonexistent.

As you might be able to conclude, my experience with the New York Life training program prepared me for the countless scenarios that would unfold at kitchen tables and business offices for the next three-plus years. Sure, I learned how to succeed at selling financial products, but I was also better prepared to market the future of this nation to my constituents and colleagues in the Senate.

WHEN THE COLD CALL BECOMES THE GOLDEN CALL

Listen, there are limited joys to cold calling. Opening up the phone book (anybody remember those?), picking up the phone, asking uninterested people to take an interest in you and your product—it's less enjoyable than going to your favorite dentist to get a cavity filled. On a day of contacting one small business after another, I randomly placed a cold call to WeMo Lawn Service, or WML. I talked with Al Jenkins, the owner of the small business, and in that first call to him, I followed the instructions as laid out by my training. The goal was not to sell anything over the phone, but simply to set up an appointment with the business owner. Thankfully, Al said yes, and we started a conversation and a friendship that would change my life.

When I met him in his small office in Goose Creek (those Gators again) in 1988, I talked for an hour about all the products and services that I thought could benefit his family and his lawn service. My proposal was thorough, and my presentation was complete. I felt polished and good about it. And then Al looked over to me and said something that changed everything. He said, "Tim, I am interested in buying some financial services products, but I am more interested in developing an understanding of who you are."

Wait a minute. That question was not part of the script in my training.

As a young salesperson, I came in there with one goal on my mind—to sell him something, anything! But with one question, Al taught me an essential approach to successful sales: a long-term view creates more sales opportunities and far more value. I started to wonder if Al had been through our training program, but he had not. He simply understood the importance of inter-personal relationships and the value of helping others.

Again, it's true in sales and it's true in politics; it's true in families, and it's true in our nation. It is always in our enlightened self-interest to put others before ourselves. This is the lesson that Al began to teach me: how I could help others without thinking of myself first.

Al Jenkins became a mentor in my life, and he became a life-long friend. Eventually I left New York Life, and I am still most thankful to that company for the gift of my start, my training, and my friendship with Al.

ULTIMATUMS IN BUSINESS

In 1991, I joined an independent insurance group in Charleston called Triest & Sholk. I was a vice president, and I sold property, casualty, health, and life insurance. I was nervous, and leads were hard to come by—we were back to cold calls, dialing for dollars. I had some practice now, but it was still grueling work. When I had been at the company for four years and my employer gave me an ulitmatum, things got even harder.

Long story short, the private doctors had a dispute with the state-employed doctors over an alleged competitive advantage based on state subsidies. A local hospital was in the middle of a tax-free bond debate with Charleston County, the council on which I had recently been elected to serve. The insurance agency I worked with insured many of the private sector doctors, and with only nine votes on the council, my vote was critical.

I had had what seemed like reasonable conversations about the pros and cons of the underlying issues with the folks at the head of my agency. Their points were compelling, and I found myself becoming persuaded. They were laser focused on what was best for the agency, but as both a salesman and a councilman, I was concerned about distinguishing between my vote and the agency's best interest.

As the agency owners, they could not imagine any of their employees voting against their clients, but I was the only county council member on the team at the agency. I immediately found myself embroiled in this controversy, the biggest issue before the county council.

My employer gave me what felt like an ultimatum. He sat behind his desk with a steely look in his eyes, and the message was clear: I could either be with the agency or against it, but there was no middle ground. I was devastated, but my decision came quickly. If you put me in a corner and tell me what I must do, I will likely do the opposite.

Within a few weeks, my keys were taken and my time as an employee at the agency came to an abrupt end. Looking back, I don't know that I necessarily disagreed with my former boss on the issue, but I had real conflict with his approach. It seems like I've always wanted to walk a road less traveled, though sometimes with fear and trepidation.

I have always been comforted by the notion that the Lord has a ram in the bush. In more familiar terms, I believe that when one door closes, another door opens. He always has a plan in the works. In the span of just a few short months, I went from top of the mountain to the valley and then back up again. I met a successful Allstate agency owner name Ron, and we hit it off. While my former employer was never really a fan of my political work, Ron embraced politics and opened his agency to me. By the end of the year, I had landed in a position that paid more and opened the doors for real opportunity. I joined the team at Allstate, and that's where I invested the majority of my business career.

I had that entrepreneur fire blazing within me, and I wanted to own an agency within the company, but Allstate wasn't so sure. The first time I applied, they told me no. I stayed after it, I kept showing up and honing my skill, and when I applied again a few months later, this time they accepted me. But, consistent with the patterns in my life, I had to go through some hard times before the good ones came. The first week after I opened my own agency, we made exactly zero sales. Nothing, nada, zilch. I had become so focused on selling that I forgot what grounded me. I lost track of what had given me the clarity I needed in order to succeed—my faith.

So, I invited my Pastor Greg Surratt over to the agency, and we prayed together. How had I forgotten to pray about this endeavor?

Just like everything else in my life, my business belonged to God first. I wanted to honor Him through the way I ran my business. I knew it in my heart, but my head had muddied the waters through all the stress of needing success. Once we were centered and refocused, the sales began to come.

We came up with a marketing plan focused on selling homeowner's insurance, and we worked hard to make inroads with closing attorneys, real estate agents, and mortgage brokers. We tried a unique approach; we promised folks we would provide them with a quote within one hour of receiving a request. With that promise in place, our sales went through the roof. How amazing that simply giving someone an answer could be the catalyst and power to our success. It absolutely kicked things off for us.

There were about a dozen Allstate agents around the state who opened their agencies the same time we did, and Allstate has a competition between all agencies that open at the same time. After thirteen weeks, we were on top. Eight months after I opened my agency in 1999, I was awarded New Agency Owner of the Year in South Carolina. That rejection years before had been just one more roadblock in my path, but I did not let it stop me. Allstate taught me yet again that America is the land of second chances.

As I continued with Allstate, I began to discover the specific success that leads to you signing your name on the front of the check instead of the back—the difference between receiving a paycheck and the freedom to write one. The company awarded trips and vacations to the top salespeople at the end of each year, and I earned a trip to Australia. I remember feeling on top of the world as I visited the Land Down Under. Me, a poor kid from North Charleston, had found success to the point where one of the biggest companies in the world had flown me halfway across the globe as a reward for my hard work. Those long hours at the office, the cold calls, the hard days, and the learning curves—they had all paid off.

I am forever glad that I chose to pursue the sales path instead of becoming an attorney. That decision has given me the experience of running businesses, gaining real-world skills, and earning common sense. (I'm not suggesting lawyers can't have common sense, just that sometimes it's harder to find.)

STARTING A NONPROFIT

My accomplishments at Allstate laid the foundation for me to try other things. I opened a real estate company, and established a small business that was a not for profit venture to help people struggling with cancer. I launched this organization with my friend Wendy, after she had her own life-threatening brush with the disease. Her story is absolutely amazing—her boyfriend's dog jumped on her chest and left a bruise that wouldn't go away. She was annoyed by the dog and bothered by the bruise, and then she felt a hard lump underneath her right breast. Her doctor initially thought the lump was a hematoma from the collision with the dog, but further exams and a biopsy concluded that Wendy had an aggressive tumor. When the dog jumped on her, he bumped the tumor into a nerve ending, bringing it to her attention. The doctor concluded that the dog may have saved her life. Wendy continues to celebrate her remission with a painting of Jake the dog in her home, a reminder that blessings come in all shapes and sizes, and some angels have four legs.

The success of our business was personally important to both Wendy and me, but we started with no hopes of making a profit. As is often the case with the best things in life, the goal was far greater than money and more precious than gold. Wendy had a contagious and motivating passion to help women who were battling breast cancer, and she was excited to help other women face the challenges she had known. For example, when she had undergone chemo and radiation, she found it nearly unbearable to drive her car due to the pressure on her chest from the seat belt. One of the products that she developed and we marketed was a seat belt harness that would provide more cushion for brittle skin that can result from cancer treatments. The development of the seat belt cushion offered her more comfort and better focus on the road, and we helped countless women to find the same.

When she approached me about teaming up to provide skin care products to address the challenges of cancer treatments, I was an absolute yes. She developed soaps and creams made from goat milk to cleanse and comfort the patients during the treatments. Wendy told me that she had found a number of helpful creams on the internet, but there was no place to order them in person. We made that possible, and I like to say that when Wendy approached me with her ideas, I was sitting on a yes. I was so excited to be able to help her move her dreams forward, and what a joy it was to invest in a company that would truly make a difference in people's lives.

In the same way that I worked to help better people's lives through projects such as my business with Wendy, I also made it a point to hire folks from my community, to help train them and ensure they were learning new skills to make their futures brighter. I wanted to help them, but I also wanted to equip them to find success on their own.

Our Allstate agency was located about a mile from the Citadel Mall in Charleston, and I bought most of my clothes at the

Dillard's inside that mall. After shopping there a few times, I met a Hispanic saleswoman named Margaret, and I could tell there was something different about her. Margaret was a military spouse and mother, and she was exceedingly kind and skilled at her work. Since she already lived in the area, she had a vested interest in the success of her neighbors as well as her own.

I knew that Allstate was expanding their market in the Hispanic community, and we had been working to find a bilingual employee. The job paid a good salary and offered some stability, and we certainly could have brought in candidates from throughout the tri-county area to fill the position. After all, it's easier to hire people from other parts of town where opportunities are more available, and therefore the people are already trained. Of course, she knew absolutely nothing about insurance; let's face it, most people who work outside the insurance industry know very little beyond the basics. But I did not care about what skills Margaret lacked. I wanted to unleash the potential that she absolutely held. So, we hired her. Interestingly, Margaret met me the same way I met the manager of New York Life—through successful sales in a clothing store.

She worked for me for years and years. Her husband got a job transfer that required them to move, so I lost that great employee—but I did not lose that great friend. We are still in touch to this day, and her employment opportunity in my office gave her a chance to build a skill set that would lead to more personal success.

OPPORTUNITY ZONES
Part of my success at Allstate and the other companies I started came from something I think entrepreneurs and small businesses

across the country would be well served to do, and something I
have championed in Congress as well: invest in the potential of
the people. This experience with Margaret is an example of the
fruit of Opportunity Zones, of investing in the people within a
community where they live. As I have mentioned, I learned some
of my best communication skills through my experiences in the
sales force, and yes, I learned that it's easier to hire people from
out of town who are already trained, or even to find employees
from parts of town where more opportunities are made available to them. But to truly rebuild our most vulnerable communities, one of our focuses must be on taking advantage of the
massive potential of the people already living there. That's also
the concept behind the Opportunity Zones program. It directly
targets private investments to distressed communities that have
been named Opportunity Zones, where more than 30 million
Americans live.

Prevailing wisdom has always said that government intervention is what helps impoverished communities, but I have taken
a stand against that belief. Instead, I believe private businesses
should help these communities by investing in them. As you know
by now, I tend to go against the grain, and I like to think outside
the box. This plan for Opportunity Zones has challenged everyone's ideas on how to fix the problem of poverty, and the success
is both unprecedented and undeniable.

My mom and my grandparents were great examples for me.
They had the will to kick the door down, but they did not have
the key to unlock opportunity. With a fair chance, they could
have done anything, and there are millions of people like that
in thousands of communities across the country. The federal
government can only do so much in that area. It is up to the people

and local communities to make this a priority. My dream is to equip these people with the tools to find success in their finances, businesses, educations, and families—by giving them the key to unlock opportunity.

"When written in Chinese, the word 'crisis' is composed of two characters. One represents danger and the other represents opportunity."

—JOHN F. KENNEDY

CHAPTER 8

OPPORTUNITIES IN WINNING AND IN LOSING

THE BUTTERFLIES in my stomach felt like they had the wings of eagles as I walked into the Charleston County Republican Party meeting in July 1994. I had decided that I was going to announce my candidacy for a seat on Charleston County Council. I saw the familiar faces of some people I had spoken with over the past few days, and I saw a whole bunch of folks I did not know. I stepped to the microphone, and I delivered my speech about the importance of economic development in the face of the naval base closure, the creation of a new industrial park to spur more private sector activity in commerce, and our personal responsibility. I closed by talking about how we could succeed together. My specific proposal was to work toward creating a Class A Industrial Park, and in the end, that is what we accomplished. Today, the complex has twenty-five companies providing good jobs and good tax revenue.

The audience response was positive to my pitch, save one critical point. An official stood up and said, "Tim I appreciate your willingness to run, but you do know that there has never been a black person elected as a Republican for anything in Charleston County?"

My response was quick and simple. "No, I did not know that, but ultimately, we are better together. This run presents the best opportunity to serve." I was confident and clear in my words, but what was actually running through my mind was the realization that I might be the only person in the room who thought I could win.

I knew in my heart that it was time to take that step forward, to accept the responsibility of building a brighter future, not for my own family, but for my community as a whole. I had a long history of campaigning for the chance to lead—all the way back to high school.

A FAILING FRESHMAN BECOMES A LEADER

Even as I was failing out of school during my freshman year, my teachers recognized kernels of leadership skills taking root beneath my antics as class clown. The year before that, my eighth-grade teacher, Mrs. Edgeworth, encouraged me to harness my talkative nature and get involved in student council. Because of her, I ran my first successful political race in the eighth grade. So, when the student council race came around during my freshman year at Stall High, I was fortunate and thankful to be elected vice president of the freshman class.

A lot of people roll their eyes when they talk about student council being life-changing for them, but it was absolutely anchoring for me. Yes, even though I was unable to pass English, Spanish, World Geography, and Civics, I was still eligible to be the vice president of the freshman class. This makes me laugh now, and it may tell us all we need to know about the minimal role our student council played that year, but I was thrilled to be given the opportunity. The Student Council Association made me a part of something important. I found a sense of belonging that was outside of sports.

I believe it is critical for high schoolers to start understanding the significance of their role in the civic responsibilities of their city, state, and our nation. So many kids are looking for somewhere they can be themselves, and without that safe place, their sense of alienation drives them to bad behavior. Students today face so many challenges we never had to think about, whether it be pressure from social media or learning new technologies. So, it is all the more important to make sure our kids have a place where they can express themselves and not have to worry about being rejected.

Balancing student council, schoolwork (or my lack thereof), and football was certainly challenging, but I found my way. My teachers appreciated my willingness to be constructive, and my fellow students seemed comfortable bringing their problems to me. Case in point: by the time I reached my senior year, I was chosen as the "Most Dependable."

Let me clarify: this was obviously not because I was on time, because I was never on time. (Even today that holds true. Just ask the Transportation Security Administration workers at any airport as I rush to catch my plane. Thank God for pre-check!) It was also not because I maintained perfect attendance, because I missed plenty of days (though never for nefarious purposes—to be clear!).

No, I was named Most Dependable because of my willingness to help others, and the fact that it seemed to be what I was born to do. I didn't drink alcohol or party at all; in fact, I became the kid that my friends relied on. Dependability is a simple value, but it was difficult to maintain, not because it made my life harder, but because I placed so much pressure on myself to try to help anyone in need. By the time my mentor John Moniz started teaching me the lesson of enlightened self-interest, the concept that it is better to give than receive, he was in fact reinforcing what I had learned in school, even if I had not recognized it yet.

That lesson came straight from the Bible and from my grandmother. She taught me the words of Luke 6:38: *"Give, and it will be given to you. A good measure, pressed down, shaken together and running over, will be poured into your lap. For with the measure you use, it will be measured to you."* That has absolutely been my experience. It's not a "get-rich-quick scheme," but I have found that when you give your best to others, they give their best to you. The blessings are not what we get in return, but the return comes from a sense of gratitude that is immeasurable. And as a freshman who was academically lost and emotionally wandering, I was grounded by a call to help my classmates with their issues. It wasn't necessarily an official task in my role as the vice president of the freshman class; it was simply a strong, insatiable desire within me to assist others.

THE MAN WHO THINKS HE CAN

During my sophomore year, I didn't serve in any office, but I entered the scene again in my junior year when I became the vice president of the Student Government Association, or SGA, and in my senior year I was elected president. This was a significant win again, because it helped me to define my purpose. In a racially diverse school, there will always be opportunities for folks to segregate back into their familiar, imagined pools, and I had the opportunity to bring a diverse group of people back together to discuss some of the challenges we were facing.

Miss Davis, my high school principal, gave us opportunities to dive into real issues, from plans for improving the schoolwork experience, to dealing with the distracting heat during the warmer months of the school year—September through November, and April through June. We did not have air-conditioning in our classrooms, and it was far more challenging to focus in the sweltering South Carolina heat. Tackling these relevant issues, as well as being an athlete on the track and football teams, were the primary reasons why I was selected to go to Boys' State, a nationwide program where teachers, administrators, and students from schools across individual states choose two rising seniors to attend a week-long government simulation course, similar to Model UN. It's quite an experience that very few high schoolers get the chance to have.

When I attended in 1982, I participated with a group of guys from all across South Carolina, an incredibly impressive crew who were very motivated to succeed. Over my seven days there, I grew closer to those guys than I did with some people whom I had known for years. Very quickly, I understood the importance of getting along with people who are not like me, and I learned that everyone—and I do mean everyone—has untapped potential. Part of the journey of Boys' State is to figure out how to extract the leadership qualities hiding just below the surface of each of us. It's an opportunity to challenge ourselves in areas where we may be uncomfortable. For me, that meant learning how to successfully run for governor at Boys' State.

I still remember my speech as I tried to bring that victory home, and I wish I could tell you it was impressive. It was not. My goal was to share with everyone why they should be excited about their future, and that if you think you can win, then you can win. I recited a poem called "The Man Who Thinks He Can" by Walter Wintle. The first stanza reads,

If you think you are beaten, you are,
If you think you dare not, you don't,
If you like to win, but you think you can't,
It's almost a "cinch" you won't.
If you think you'll lose, you've lost,
For out in the world you find
Success begins with a fellow's will;
It's all in the state of mind.

It was a great poem, but unfortunately my delivery was pretty flat. It's an unforgettable key to public speaking: one must always be able to successfully communicate not only the point, but also the essence of the speech. Whether you are running for office or simply trying to motivate someone in need, the whole package requires a lot more than simply the right words; it requires the right delivery, the right emotions, and the right focus.

I can see now what I got wrong at Boys' State that day: I did not feel prepared. That first speech made me feel inadequate, and then brought the dreaded stomach full of butterflies. Knowing that feeling served me well when I began running for elected office in the real world over a decade later. I had learned that success as a public servant has less to do with who you are, and more to do with who you want to serve. Those butterflies forced me to prepare better, to become more knowledgeable, and to find better solutions to be the best I can be for the people I serve.

The nerves still come today whenever I am preparing to go on television or speak on an issue. The butterflies don't disappear, but they do get smaller and the opportunity for success grows larger. The fastest way to succeed is to make sure that it's not about me. When the focus is on me, then it blurs my vision. But when the focus is on others, it becomes much easier to succeed.

I don't remember who won the governor's race at Boys' State that day, but I know that it wasn't me. My biggest victory at that point was in defeat, an experience I would encounter over and over again. I don't recommend losing as a way to learn valuable lessons, but for me, it's been unavoidable. Defeat often opens our eyes to the experiences that we may not have otherwise seen. I continue to drive up to Anderson, South Carolina, to speak at Boys' State every year, in part as a thank-you for the ways that organization changed my life.

THE ULTIMATE PRESENTATION

Without question, public service is about serving constituents, and running for office is perhaps the ultimate sales presentation. I believe that an important part of that equation is having a marketing strategy that represents an authentic and sincere view of who you are and what you plan to do for your constituents. Voters ultimately look for the best candidate to represent them, and I find the best way to meet that expectation is to run in the same spirit as you would like to serve.

During the spring of 1990, when I was twenty-four years old, the federal credit union where I banked was preparing to elect new members for their board of directors. I cannot recall exactly why I thought I was the best fit as a twenty-four-year-old, but I was in. And my first task was to collect the signatures of 250 members of the credit union. I started with Joe McKeown, a friend of mine and an employee at Health Quest, the gym where I worked out. I walked into the gym, clipboard in hand, looking for any of my friends who were members of the Heritage Trust Federal Credit Union. Joe was the first to sign, and I spent weeks interrupting people as they worked out. I visited other places I often frequented—restaurants, other gyms, the mall, and my apartment complex. I went after those signatures like a dog goes after a bone, and a lot of people turned me down. At one point I was at my favorite restaurant, California Dreaming, having lunch with clipboard in tow. As I walked out, I ran into a friend of mine, and I explained to him that I was trying my best to garner the necessary signatures for my campaign. He too was a member of the Heritage Trust, so naturally I asked him to sign the petition. He said no, he would not! *Ouch!*

Despite some painful encounters like that one, I garnered the signatures I needed, and later that year, I became a member of the Heritage Trust board of directors. My role on the board of directors turned out to be an amazing experience for me, a young man interested in finance, and—more important—interested in serving my community. I found ways to improve the quality of financial literacy within my community, and hopefully helped people find employment within the financial services industry.

As I served, I kept in mind the personal mission that I adopted at the time of John Moniz's death—to positively impact the lives of one billion people. This was a step, perhaps a small step, but a very important first step in the right direction of realizing that goal just four years after John Moniz's sudden death. I loved the mission of the credit union, which has always been to serve the under-served. This message would reverberate throughout my political career, and may have served as the first brick in my Opportunity Agenda, focused on helping people who have been left behind.

My role on the board was also an important early step in the direction of running for public office in Charleston County, and I served for seven years with Heritage Trust before resigning to avoid any perceived conflicts. I took my first steps into the true political world as a campaign volunteer for Republican Mark Sanford for Congress in 1994. When I joined Mark's campaign,

I believe he was sitting between 2 and 4 percent in the polls. He was not slated to win. Back then, Mark Sanford was a new kind of Republican. He was environmentally friendly, young, photogenic, driven by a real passion to serve, and he committed to only serving three two-year terms. In an interesting twist of events, he ultimately succeeded over the favorite, Van Hipp. Amazingly, he ultimately won in a runoff, and it was exciting to be a part of this historic campaign.

At the same time Mark was winning his race for Congress, the chairman of the Charleston County Council, Keith Summey, was in a race to become the next mayor of my hometown, North Charleston. The combination of watching Keith's campaign and working on Mark's gave me valuable insights about the grittiness of politics. The glamorous life of a candidate is well overstated. It seemed like an endless battle as a volunteer knocking on the doors, and I later learned on the federal level that it cost millions of dollars to get the campaign message into the homes of likely voters. I learned that process as a grunt, by walking door to door, sharing Mark's information, attending events, and talking to potential voters.

The lessons I learned on the campaign trail for Mark would transfer seamlessly for me and my run for county council. Even though I felt like a conservative, and even though I had worked on Mark's campaign, most of my black friends and associates were Democrats. As a newcomer to the scene, I figured I would meet with both parties, and I would gauge their response to my potentially running for office.

I decided to attend the county Democratic convention in 1994, and once there I approached a state senator and shared my desire to run for county council in the seat that was recently vacated. His response was somewhat surprising. He told me, "Son, you're going to wait your turn and get in line. You can't just walk in the front door and jump in front of people who've been serving for years and waiting for their chance."

He struck the killer blow, and tacked on to the end, "Son, you'll just have to be patient."

I have never had an overwhelming supply of patience. To be told I needed to practice it, and to be dismissed? This was not what I wanted to hear. I was building my insurance business, I had honed my skills on the credit union board, and I had earned my college degree in political science. I was ready. While I appreciate the important role of committees and seniority in the party, I had a passion that was burning strong for public service. I was confident my vision for our community would be shared by the constituents of Charleston County.

So, I went to the Republican Party meeting at North Charleston City Hall on a Monday evening to talk with the Republican Party about my candidacy. I told a room full of voters that I was passionate about being a difference maker. Even though I wasn't a terribly smooth speaker, I think the party saw a willing candidate with the energy and the enthusiasm to run—and maybe even make history—along the way. It wasn't until I sat in my car, excited and nervous after the meeting, that it dawned on me: I had just given my first official political speech. It was choppy, short, but full of compassion, energy, and vision.

The Republican Party seemed very positive, and the overall response was, "Run, Tim, run!" One official told me I could not win, but most of them said, "Yes, we would love to see you run!" That was refreshing, especially after my visit to the Democrat Party resulted in comments like, "You can't run. It's not your time. Get in line, and the day will come when your bid for elective office will be an option. It's not today."

Looking back now, it's pretty clear the Democratic Party would have had some qualms with my policy positions anyway, but at the time it made sense to visit both parties. Telling me I had a chance was all I needed. Yes, I was twenty-nine, but I had a vision for my community and I didn't appreciate being told by the Democrats to stand at the back of the line. I wanted the voters to decide my fate, not the political elite. Never mind that nearly 300,000 people lived in Charleston County. I would meet as many of them as possible to share a vision of our future. The one thing I've always known in life is that I can't do it alone, and success cannot come without the assistance of others.

It always takes a team of true believers to win over skeptics who in their hearts want to believe. After that meeting, Chairman Mark Hartley, Cyndi Mosteller, Terrye Seckinger, and Cindy Costa jumped in with support for me early on. I am so thankful for those people, and they still remain wonderful supporters today.

In my county council race, I learned one major difference between the local and federal level—it was the candidate who spent more time knocking on doors and asking directly for votes. I would stuff envelopes with a handful of volunteers, and we worked into the wee hours of the morning to finish the trifold or single 5x7 cards presenting my short agenda. I was the one calling the printer to get a lower price on bulk mailings, and I was the one learning about bulk rates at the post office versus first-class postage.

This was 1994, and with the nation experiencing Bill Clinton's lurch to the left, the Republican Party, led by Newt Gingrich and Jack Kemp, responded with the Contract with America. The success of this campaign and contract would lead to the Republican Party regaining control of the United States House of Representatives for the first time in forty years.

Meanwhile, in Charleston County I was running my first race and I had the privilege of meeting Jack Kemp and Newt Gingrich at the Elks Lodge in Charleston. I was starstruck by Jack Kemp, who has always been the model of conservatism for me. He was a former NFL quarterback with a gift for gab and a passion for economics. The only thing that exceeded his passion for economics was his passion for people. We remember him for his work in Congress or role as secretary of housing and urban development; however, it was his passion for people that landed him the position of secretary. I was excited to see Jack and Newt reinvigorate conservatism at the federal level as I started my journey at the local level.

This was a critical time not just for the nation as a whole, but for Charleston County in particular. Now the entire world knows how great a place Charleston is to live and eat (with Greenville opening just as many eyes these days as well!), but in 1994, the words "tourism" and "eating" were not synonymous with Charleston. We were a military town—no "ifs, ands, or buts" about it. The Charleston Naval Complex and Joint Base Charleston ensured that all the branches of the military were stationed in Charleston, with the Navy's presence being the biggest.

In 1993, the federal government had passed a new round of Base Realignment and Closure (BRAC), and its new provisions devastated the Charleston Naval Base. At its height, tens of thousands of jobs relied on the naval shipyards and the related facilities. It anchored the Chicora-Cherokee neighborhood and had sent ships up and down the Cooper River since 1901. While the writing on the wall had perhaps been obvious for a while, we were still devastated.

The Chicora-Cherokee neighborhood is still struggling today; I kick-started my National Opportunity Zone tour there in 2018 in

part because of the story those people have to tell. It was a booming community when the naval base was operating, and they were
unable to financially adjust after the base's closure. That community has a special place in my heart, as my granddaddy lived in
this neighborhood for more than thirty years.

As a community, we were in shock. Was this possible, when
our two senators, Strom Thurmond and Fritz Hollings, were two
of the longest-tenured members of the Senate? It was simply unbe-
lievable. How do you replace those jobs, that tax base, and the loss
of what some would see as the heart of our community? It was
without a doubt the worst news our city had ever faced. Our team
would go door-to-door for weeks and weeks on end. We knew that
Charleston was going to have to adapt or die.

John Moniz had taught me to focus on what I can control, and
while I couldn't control the naval base closing, I could control how
I responded. We campaigned on creating a Class A office complex
and a renewed focus on economic development. A Class A industrial park is a business development area that provides synergy
and opportunity for businesses to collaborate, coordinate, and
celebrate the successes to come out of the park. I viewed our
community almost like the baseball field in *Field of Dreams*—if
we build it, they will come. At the time of my first campaign we
did not have one, and now we have a successful footprint with
internationally known companies.

I also campaigned on a core value that has remained central
in every campaign I have run since: personal responsibility. That
is a rather odd issue to focus on in a county council race, but I did
not care. Washington was a mess, and people's faith was low—not
just in their government, but in some of the people running it. I
wanted everyone to know that I believed in individual responsibility, not just for the people I hoped to represent, but for myself

as well. We raised a hefty amount of money, nearly $25,000. At the time, that seemed like $1 billion.

I remember the day before Christmas Eve in 1994, Joe McKeown and I met with the then-chairman of the South Carolina Republican Party, Henry McMaster. You might know him better now as the governor of South Carolina. We got to the meeting with Henry and some of his staff, including Trey Walker, executive director at the time, now the governor's chief of staff, and Chris Neely, who was chair and recently started a school for children with special needs. We ran through what I now know are just typical questions, like, "What are your positions on XYZ? What do you hope to accomplish?" He asked me those, but the last one stuck out. Henry asked, "Tim, why are you running?"

I told him my mission. "I want to positively affect the lives of a billion people with a message of hope and opportunity before I die."

Henry pushed his chair back. He looked at Joe, then at his staff, and then at me. And he said, "I think you're gonna win!"

ON THE CAMPAIGN TRAIL

As I mentioned, I learned that when you're running for local office, the candidate knocks on more doors than his individual supporters do. I must have personally knocked on 2,000 doors. My name recognition was near zero. Yes, I was serving on the federal credit union board, I was starting my insurance career, and I went to school in Charleston—but nonetheless, I had a lot of work to do to build my name ID.

How do you do that when you have limited campaign funds? Sweat equity! This was a special election, and turnout is low in special elections, so the approach is simple: the candidate who gets his supporters to the polls on Election Day will win. The biggest mistake I could make is not getting my friends to the polls! So, I made a list of everyone I knew in the county—and I mean *everyone*, just like I had when I was starting my insurance career with New York Life Insurance Company. I called them over the summer, and again in the fall. I said hello again in January, and then I contacted them one more time in February in the week before the special election. Back then, there was no texting or emailing, so it was a very time-consuming process.

I purchased radio advertising during the month before the election. Former congressman Arthur Ravenel publicly endorsed me, and he recorded a radio spot for me ending in his famous "thank you." So many people are still commenting to me about that radio spot even now, years afterward. It was a great boost for the campaign.

In response to our December meeting with Henry McMaster, the state party committed $5,000 toward a direct mail piece. This was a big boost, because at that time, county council members ran county-wide, as opposed to single-member districts. In other words, residents living almost ninety miles apart would vote in this election. That is a lot of mailboxes to hit! I so appreciated the financial support from the state party. My team and I had laid the groundwork for a successful outcome, and the party's $5,000 gave us one final push.

COUNTY COUNCIL, HERE WE COME

After six months of campaigning, it was finally the moment we had been waiting for: election night, February 7, 1995. We won with 73 percent of the vote. That is huge! A 73 percent win, for a guy who heard from one party that it would be best to stand at the back of the line, and for the other party, who said I might have a chance to win. I knew that folks had put their trust in me to help lead an economic renaissance in Charleston, and it was time to get to work.

The shipyard had been part of the fabric of our community for decades, and we thought it would continue to be part of our future. But BRAC had changed everything. We could either react negatively or respond positively to the bad news that we had received about the closing of the base. I knew that we were Charlestonians, and if we made up our minds, we could respond positively. We could reuse the property alongside the port to re-create ourselves.

This theme has emerged throughout my life in public service. It seems that challenges precede opportunities and tragedy gives way to triumph if you don't quit. Charleston did not quit; we went to work! I'll never forget the advertising campaign where we had our newly created economic development alliance. We crafted a picture that said Charleston was open for business. It was a man in a suit with his pant legs rolled up to his knees, his laptop in his hands. He said, "With sunshine, water, and sand, Charleston is a place you'd want to live, work, and play." He was 100 percent correct.

Since the dire reports of the demise of Charleston, we have seen a 33 percent increase in our population, and we have become the number one tourist destination in America for the last four years, according to *Condé Nast Traveler* magazine. Furthermore, incomes have increased substantially, quality of life is up exponentially, and the southern charm that is well known in the Holy City remains intact.

On election night, we celebrated at T-bones restaurant, and I received calls from Governor David Beasley, Senator Strom Thurmond, and so many other South Carolina political luminaries. The newspaper touted my election as the first black Republican since Reconstruction to win a seat county-wide, and I then became the first African-American Republican to win a county seat anywhere in South Carolina.

This started a string of similar firsts, something I was a little uneasy talking about. On one hand, I completely understand the significance of a person of color achieving something never done before. Winning a seat county-wide as a black Republican said a lot about how far we had come as a community where the Civil War started. That kind of a win shows kids with a childhood like mine that there is a path to achieve your dreams, and I hope it brings a different perspective to the party as a whole. But on the other hand, I was not elected because I was black. I was elected because people believed in my positions, and they knew that I cared about making their lives better. I believe in the American people and was only encouraged when some folks told me I had no chance to win.

It is amazing how many things we fail to attempt because someone else tells us we can't. Whether that's getting an A on a test, going for a promotion at work, running for political office, or any goal you set your mind to, other people will always have an opinion on your future. Too often, our leaders in government fall into the same trap. They'll say, "You can't do this, because it's never been done. You can't say that because you'll lose. You need to do this because an important person says to."

Do you know what I say? Sometimes, losing and doing the right thing are the best path forward.

*"Courage is the greatest of all virtues,
because if you haven't courage, you
may not have an opportunity to use
any of the others."*

—SAMUEL JOHNSON

CHAPTER 9

LOSING, AND BOUNCING BACK

TRY AND TRY AGAIN

ABC's *Wide World of Sports* used to have an intro about the thrill of victory and the agony of defeat. I remember watching those images over and over as a kid. You would see these amazing athletes surfing, riding a bucking bronco, or skiing down a mountain, and then being swamped under a massive wave, or thrashing back and forth across the ground when the bronco bucked them off, or hitting everything on their painful track down the mountain.

While I was riding high on the thrill of victory, I was not particularly concerned with the agony of defeat. With that in mind, and buoyed by my big victory in the race for a seat on Charleston County Council, I ran for office again just twelve months later. I gave up my seat on county council for a long-shot effort at the state senate.

I decided to challenge South Carolina state senator Robert Ford, a Democrat who represented a district that had been gerrymandered so that it was heavily Democratic.

As I went through the process of deciding to run, I remember praying with one of my prayer partners, Brandt Shelbourne.

Despite the challenges, we both agreed it was obvious that I should run, and I'll never forget what he said at the end of our prayer: "Tim, the Lord may have called you to run . . . but that doesn't necessarily mean to win."

That turned out to be quite prophetic. I lost. But it didn't take a prophet to see the writing on the wall; I knew it, and he knew it. There is no real political analysis necessary to explain what happened; I just got beaten. When I look back now, I see that it taught me another lesson I needed to learn. The decision to run showed me that I had to trust my instincts, even if the end result was not what I wanted.

On election night, when a reporter asked me about my decision, I told him that losing was not actually a defeat, just a delay. And while many folks throughout history have probably thought the same thing, I was determined I would actually make that true. For the next few months, I focused on growing my business and I continued studying the issues that were affecting the county.

In 1997, there was an election to fill a recently vacated seat on the county council. I had the chance to restart my career in public service, and I was going to take it. I remember this election as well as any, as my reelection to the council was far from a sure thing. It is unspeakably difficult to lose a race, and then come back and win again. I had been out of public office for over a year, and election night was intense and emotional. Thankfully, I won. My career in public service was back on track.

OUTNUMBERED

Two years later, I was invited to be a guest on Bill Maher's show *Politically Incorrect*. For a local elected official, the chance to join a national television show was a big deal, and I was excited about the chance to go. That week's show centered on Martin Luther

King Jr. Day, and I accepted their invitation to join the show as the "outnumbered" guest. Basically, that meant it was going to be me against everyone else.

The panel included Chuck D from the influential hip-hop group Public Enemy, two other liberal guests, and me. If you have ever listened to Public Enemy, you know that Chuck D has no problem saying what he really means—no matter how iconoclastic.

Throughout our history, the story of America includes redemption. There's a reason why, at Senator Robert Byrd's funeral, U.S. Senate chaplain Barry Black preached his eulogy. For many years, Senator Robert Byrd was a member of the Ku Klux Klan, and Barry Black isn't just named Black, he is black. Think of the transformation that had to happen in Senator Byrd's life for him to ask an African-American to preach at his funeral. That is redemption, and this kind of redemption is a huge part of the story of America. It is hard to hate what you know, and it is certainly hard to hate what you know up close.

The show got interesting when Maher asked me a question about Strom Thurmond and his history and legacy in South Carolina. I responded with the truth: that I served as the vice chairman of Thurmond's last election in 1996. To be clear, I would not have been the vice chair of his 1966 election, thirty years earlier, because at that point his transformation had not yet occurred.

Bill Maher just about turned white as a ghost, and he started yelling. This may not be much of a surprise now, but back then, he was a bit more moderated in the tone of his voice (but not in his political agenda).

To say that he was shocked, fascinated, and disappointed that there was a black person who would support a former segregationist would be an understatement. Honestly, it is easy to see why he would say that on the surface, but our nation's story runs so much deeper than that.

I explained to Maher that not only had I supported Senator Thurmond's reelection, but that he earned the votes of nearly 30 percent of the black voters in South Carolina as well.

Today, there's no doubt that in every industry, every institution, and certainly in every community of faith, growth and perspective are necessary. I've seen firsthand the very people who were racially biased against me, how they have changed over time, and then later approached me and apologized. I'm not suggesting that we should ever condone discrimination, but rather we should look in the mirror to first recognize our own prejudices and biases. The gift of self-awareness is one seldom opened. When we approach those who may be opposed to us or to our position with a willingness to listen, to hear instead of just respond, we may change their views of us or, frankly, our views of them.

With that in mind, I tried to explain my position as a guest on Bill Maher's show. Bill was not listening, and I learned a simple, valuable lesson: If you want to be different, be prepared to defend it at a higher level. Our nation has had to defend *who* we are and *why* we are different in so many ways throughout our history. That's the truth, and it will continue to be our burden. It's the burden of leadership and of influence. It is the burden to be in the minority and to stand firm for your unpopular position. As a guest on *Politically Incorrect,* I learned a lot about carrying the burden.

HUMILITY AS A SERVANT LEADER

When I returned home to Charleston from Los Angeles, my pastor, Greg Surratt, was kind enough to recognize me and acknowledge my appearance on *Politically Incorrect.* I stood up, graciously waving and acknowledging his kind remarks, but very quickly

I felt something stir in my own heart. This recognition could become toxic to my spirit if I was not proactive against the poison of pride.

You see, national recognition can be infectious, and it would be important to keep the focus not on me, but on the mission I was passionately pursuing. Then, an important question flew into my mind, as if the Lord were speaking to me, asking me directly: *Tim, would you enjoy serving the Lord in private as much as you enjoy serving Him in public, to the applause of so many?*

I knew I needed to do something, to act fast to keep my spirit in check. The next thought that ran through my mind was this: "Why don't you clean the bathrooms at your church?"

What? I thought. *I don't even use the bathrooms at church very often, so why in the world would I want to clean the bathrooms at the church?*

The answer was one word: humility.

I contacted the janitorial staff and volunteered to spend hours cleaning the bathrooms. My church had around two thousand people in the congregation at that time, so there were a lot of bathrooms to clean. One of the most important reminders was to respect and appreciate everyone for every job, no matter the pay or the circumstances. There is dignity in all work, no matter how inglorious, but some work requires a special person to do the job well. I was blessed to call on a team of custodians who did a fabulous job. The second lesson I learned was this: don't be too quick to take credit, when in fact there's no credit available. And the third, final, and most eye-opening lesson I learned? Men need to step closer to the urinals!

I walked away after my weekend duty of cleaning the bathrooms with an unwavering conviction about God's role in my life and the importance of being thankful.

A REBIRTH OF A CITY

Thankfully, while I was figuring these things out, the late 1990s and early 2000s were an amazing time for Charleston. It was the beginning of what we now see is a full-scale rebirth of the city. On county council, we brought the first company in what would turn into the massive Boeing plant to Charleston County, amazing growth began to blossom with sleepy suburbs like Mount Pleasant, and the world began to take notice that Charleston was a great place to work and live.

I was serving as chairman of the Charleston County Council's Economic Development Committee in 2004, which put me front and center in the county's job creation efforts. It's one thing to love where you live, and it is a whole other thing to pitch other people on why they should love it as well.

We targeted one project in particular, code-named Project Buffalo. Secrecy is always key around economic development projects, as you cannot allow the competing cities to get a leg up on you. Project Buffalo was a mission to bring a company called Vought-Alenia to Charleston County, as well as a new business called Global Aeronautica. These two entities would put us square in the middle of the aerospace manufacturing industry, as they built the mid and aft fuselage sections for Boeing. Basically, they designed and built the space where you sit on an airplane.

Boeing is one of the largest companies in the world, and an injection of jobs, creativity, and excitement would be absolutely huge in this decade after losing the navy shipyards. We were competing against Kinston, North Carolina, and Mobile, Alabama, and both cities were in states that had proven they could bring in large manufacturers. There was a significant amount of pressure to land this deal and bring South Carolina's new economic future to the Lowcountry.

It wasn't just Charleston that had struggled. The entire state had been wandering through an economic wilderness after the passage of the North American Free Trade Agreement (NAFTA). The Upstate, centered around Greenville and Spartanburg, had been heavily dependent on textiles, and NAFTA had nearly ended that. Thankfully, in the mid-1990s, BMW opened a plant in Spartanburg County that became the sparkplug for a manufacturing renaissance in our state. It is now the largest BMW plant in the world.

The Upstate was building cars, and if we landed Vought-Alenia and Global Aeronautica, the Lowcountry would be building airplanes. In December 2004, that's exactly what we did. A huge win for South Carolina!

Just over a year later, Boeing announced they were buying the two companies out and bringing the manufacturing back in house. Today, tens of thousands of jobs in the tri-county area are Boeing related, and South Carolina has become an aerospace hub. Our technical training programs have boomed, talent is flowing into the state, and we are known worldwide as a major player in the United States' manufacturing sector.

It was an honor to play such an exciting role in the transformation of my local economy, as well as in our state as a whole. I served on county council for nearly fourteen years in total, including a time as chairman, working on everything from improving our recycling program, to helping residents with potholes, to bringing thousands of new jobs to Charleston. Luckily, kind of, that time had one more lesson left to teach me.

STATE TREASURER

Soon I had my first view of the magnitude of running for statewide office. In 2007, Governor Sanford asked me if I was interested in being state treasurer. The current treasurer had been indicted, and they needed someone to take the position until the next election could be held. This would require confirmation by the state legislature, and anyone who follows South Carolina politics knows that Mark Sanford and the legislature mixed about as well as oil and water.

In 2004, the governor walked into the legislature carrying two pigs to make a point about pork in the state budget. Governor Sanford's objective was to make a point very clearly, and to do so in a provocative manner. This only served to further widen the chasm between the governor and the General Assembly. *The State* newspaper in Columbia reported:

> Others were stunned that Sanford had broken an unspoken code in South Carolina politics: We may disagree, but we avoid directly embarrassing each other.
>
> "This about tears it with the General Assembly," said Francis Marion University political scientist Neal Thigpen, a Republican. "There's no going back. They don't like being embarrassed."

That quote doesn't even address how upset they were that the pigs pooped on the carpet.

For those who knew how much of a budget hawk Sanford was, the stunt was not surprising. The response he received probably should have been an indicator to me that his nomination of me (or anyone else, for that matter) would also not go over well with the General Assembly. I was certainly aware that the legislature would choose the next treasurer, but I was more hopeful that Governor Sanford would have enough allies in the General Assembly to move my nomination forward.

Still, I was ecstatic upon receiving the initial call from the governor that he would like to nominate me to be the next treasurer of South Carolina. Of course, I was delighted to have the opportunity to serve in a position that was right up my alley. I've always loved numbers, and I'm good at them. (Notice the four subjects I failed my freshman year in high school did not include math. Math was my sweet spot.) There was no doubt I could have a positive impact, given my nearly twenty years of financial services experience and my role as a local official.

We've read before that there are two kinds of people who run for office—those who want to *be* something and those who want to *do* something. I've never run for office to have that office's title. Every time I've run for elected office, there were many things that I wanted to *do* in that role, and the treasurer's position was no different.

As the legislature was in session, I would not need to travel the entire state to introduce myself to members. I simply needed to go to the state capitol in Columbia. I was on county council at the time, and outside of the Charleston delegation, almost no one knew who I was. That said, I met Tom Davis. Tom is now a state senator, but in 2007 he was the governor's chief of staff. Tom was hopeful that he would identify one of the conservatives in the General Assembly to nominate me, and he actually suggested that I consider resigning from county council. He believed that if I resigned, it would put more pressure on the General Assembly to indeed accept the governor's nomination and vote for me to be the next treasurer.

In some ways it sounded like a good idea. I could picture it: here is this county council member who has sacrificed himself, resigned his position in order to serve his state after our treasurer has been indicted. Although the governor's desire to nominate me was supposed to be known by no one outside the governor's office, word spread—as it always does.

The Speaker of the House at that time was Bobby Harrell. Bobby is a friend of mine. He called me and told me he had caught word of the governor's plan to nominate me. Due to the way the state constitution is written in South Carolina, the Speaker of the House is frankly the most powerful elected position in the state. He commenced to tell me that the race for state treasurer was already over, and that the General Assembly had planned to vote for a state representative, Converse Chellis.

I shared with him that the governor had assured me that it would be a competitive race, and the Speaker in turn assured me that Governor Sanford was mistaken. This was a done deal. I shared the idea of my resigning from county council in order to apply more pressure to the General Assembly. He said, "Do not resign. It will not help you." He did not dissuade me from allowing the governor to nominate me, but he did not want me to make a mistake of resigning my position on county council. He stated once more that this race was over, and the treasurer would not be me.

As we approached the day of the vote, I remember asking Tom Davis if he knew who would nominate me. I didn't have a clue. Nor did he.

I was in the state capitol, and I was nervous and excited. Whatever was about to happen was indeed about to happen. I walked up a beautiful set of stairs to get to the chamber, and I felt a sense of awe as I approached the floor. I was standing in the lobby and someone came out to tell me that what the Speaker had been telling was absolutely true—the General Assembly had made up their minds, they had their guy, and they had the votes to put him in the treasurer's office.

He further told me that the smart move was to withdraw from contention. I was initially reluctant to do so, and ultimately, I decided to simply wait until the person who was going to nominate me arrived. I wanted to talk with that member and get his thoughts before making any decisions.

After what seemed like hours, it became apparent that the governor could not even find a person to nominate me. So, before the actual vote began, I withdrew my name from consideration. I think the vote count was 170–0 for Chellis. There was not even a protest vote.

There's always a silver lining in the middle of miserable situations like the one I was in. Bobby Harrell convinced me not to resign from county council. I was reluctant to do so anyway, but his counsel affirmed my political instinct. Also, in a very short period of time, I learned a lot about state politics. Just because a governor is popular with the populace does not necessarily mean he is popular with the elected officials who represent the populace.

There is nothing I could have done that would have influenced a single vote in the chamber where the person who won was one of their colleagues. Convincing someone to vote against one of their own, who was also very qualified, was a nonstarter. This process was part of the reason why I felt more prepared to run for a seat in the state House. Yes, the same body that had voted against me.

STATE HOUSE

Running for the state House, I was able to campaign in Berkeley County for the first time. This brought me into a more rural area and outside the comforts of Charleston County. My name recognition was low there, and I was running against multiple candidates who had served the county for years. Wheeler Tillman had already previously served in the South Carolina House, and Bill Crosby sat on Berkeley County Council for a dozen years. It would be tough sledding without a doubt.

The campaign presented serious challenges and required a lot of door-to-door visits, phone calls, and grassroots campaigning. One day, we walked up to a house with an old truck in the driveway. The truck had a Confederate flag bumper sticker, but I knocked on the door anyway. When I met the man who lived there, the driver of the truck with the Confederate flag, I listened without waiting to talk. Where we disagreed, I made it a point not to be disagreeable. I am sure that makes some folks reading this angry, but you know what? When we walked away, that guy had a Tim Scott sign in his front yard. Like the apostle Peter taught us, the only way to walk on water is to get out of the boat.

In South Carolina, a candidate with multiple opponents must garner 50 percent of the vote plus one in order to prevent a runoff. Avoiding a runoff would be huge, because it meant having to raise less money while avoiding a head-to-head race against someone who had represented Berkeley County previously. And you just never know what can happen in a runoff.

I had close to one hundred volunteers knocking on doors the final Saturday before the Tuesday election. These volunteers included people who were white, black, Filipino, Hispanic, and more. They included folks born in South Carolina, and folks who had recently moved there from the North. I look back so favorably at the memories of that race, not just because we won, but because of the makeup of the folks working to help me win the race. They were in the trenches with us working hard because they too were convinced that we are better together. The buzz in the air that final weekend made me believe that I would win, and maybe I could even do so without a runoff. Anyone who has ever run for office knows that feeling, and it's hard to beat!

As I have said before and I will say again, thankfully Joe ran a great campaign. We won with 53 percent of the vote, including 70 percent in Berkeley County, avoiding a runoff. There was no general election opponent, which meant I would be now spending time in Columbia a few months a year at the state House. I also became the first black Republican elected to the state legislature. A few years later, after I was elected to Congress, Bill Crosby ran for the same state House seat again, won, and served three terms.

On arriving in Columbia in early 2009, I was elected president of our freshman class. Serving in the state House also brought me in contact with people who would play significant roles in the future of my life and federal service. I could not have known then what I know now, but I am very pleased to have served with Nikki Haley, Jeff Duncan, and Mick Mulvaney, who was in the state Senate.

My first impression of Nikki was that she was fierce. Nikki, as we all know now, was born in Bamberg, South Carolina, one of the poorest areas in our state, and was successfully elected to the state House as the first Indian American woman to serve in the state General Assembly. She was, without question, one of the most conservative members of the House, making her a thorn in the side of leadership. One session she was caught in a battle with the Speaker of the South Carolina House over a committee assignment. I remember walking into a Labor, Commerce and Industry meeting and hearing that she had received a letter of her dismissal from the committee. She was outmatched and outnumbered, but unyielding. You might say she did not get confused.

She and I served together my two years in the state House, and I believe we had a healthy respect for one another. We were in different delegations, from different parts of the state, but I was able to watch her work. One of the things I observed was how focused she was, how strong she was, and that she was a woman who knew her talents exceeded her position. I believe that's one of the reasons why she decided to run for governor even as a state House representative in such a crowded primary field as the underdog—she had the intestinal fortitude to enter the race with the odds stacked against her. It proved to be a brilliant stroke of genius in so many ways.

When Nikki was elected in Bamberg, South Carolina, as an Indian American woman, this showed so very much about our great state and about her as an individual and candidate. I watched her thread the needle in the South Carolina House of Representatives, and frankly in the face of opposition, since many saw her as a challenge and therefore a problem. I saw her as someone who should have been respected and appreciated, though our circles never really came together those two years in Columbia. In many ways looking back, the pressure and the challenges that she faced in the state House proved to be the necessary training and strengthening of a gubernatorial candidate who would become the United States' ambassador to the United Nations.

Jeff Duncan came to Columbia from the Upstate and was certainly a conservative member of the body as well as a leader with a strong personality. Even though we didn't spend much time together, we had a good working relationship. He had been in the state House for years before I ever arrived, and he was more than willing to share his experience with me when necessary. We have a lot in common and share the love for football. Jeff is a die-hard Clemson fan, and was one before it was cool. As a former Tiger himself, he cheered for Clemson and was there during the glory years of the early 1980s. We were close to the same age, and

enjoyed joking with each other about our teams, as I am a dedicated South Carolina Gamecocks fan. Funnily enough, two years
after we both attended orientation for Congress two years later in
D.C., we decided to be roommates as we both made the move to
the United States House of Representatives. We ended up being
roommates for about three years, along with our Chiefs of Staff
Joe and Lance, and it was one of the better experiences of my time
in Washington.

Jeff has a passion for the outdoors as he is an avid hunter and
has a keen interest in energy policy. One of the blessings of serving in Washington with Jeff was our strengths and weaknesses
were complementary. It made us a better team as we focused
on making America the most competitive nation on earth and
making sure that South Carolina was a part of the engine.

Then comes the curious case of Mick Mulvaney. There was
not really anything curious about it. I just like making Mick sound
mysterious. As a state senator, he did not always make his way
over to the lower chamber to visit with us. But when our paths
did cross, he was always cordial, incredibly insightful, and had a
sharp sense of humor.

Mick is a good man, and he sees things in a very black-and-
white manner. He was an attorney, and, being an entrepreneur,
he knew fiscal issues very well. Even though he was in the Senate
and I was in the House, we were fighting the same fight in 2009
and 2010 working to balance the state budget. How I wish we could
get a Balanced Budget Amendment passed in Washington—God
knows we need that. Almost every single state has some kind of
balanced budget rule that prevents them from overspending, but
Washington seems to think it is immune from that sort of thinking.

Mick was a budget hawk in the state Senate, and that did not
change one bit during his time in Congress. How painful it must

be for him now as chief of staff for the president, having to come to the Hill asking for the debt ceiling to be raised—something he did not want to do as a member of Congress.

After meeting all the new faces in Columbia, I hit the ground running, working hard to keep my campaign promises to curb spending and make state government more efficient. This was during the financial crisis, and states all over the country were struggling with a drastic loss in revenue and huge deficits. We had to make tough choices, and we ended up bringing the state budget from $7 billion to $5 billion in two years. That number shows both how deep the financial crisis had hit, and perhaps how bloated our state government had become. We were required to balance the budget, and we did.

I also joined the Women's Caucus, which struck some as odd. It was clear that we did not have enough female voices in the state legislature, and I wanted to do whatever I could to help amplify the voices of those we did have. With good friends and new friends like Joan Brady, Wendy Nanney, Shannon Erickson, and Deborah Long, all members of the state House, there was no shortage of amazing women from whom to learn.

These powerful, intelligent, and strong women better equipped me to understand the challenges and the needs of women throughout South Carolina, as well as the legislative priorities of women around the state. Being raised by a single mom, I was fully acquainted with the brilliance and work ethic of women in leadership. I had watched my mom work long hours and do amazing things. As the product of a powerful single mother, my opportunity was to be a part of a caucus that would focus their attention on solving some of the issues on the minds of all women throughout South Carolina.

I will never forget marveling at how Deborah Long, an optometrist, would serve in the General Assembly, run her vibrant practice two hours away in Lancaster, and care for an ailing husband until his passing. It is hard to fully comprehend the sacrifices she was making, but her love and passion for the state were unmatched. My good friend Shannon Erickson would become a strong supporter during my run for Congress, and her energy for representing Beaufort County is boundless. She is the mom of a wonderful teenager and the wife of a full-time accountant, as well as being a business owner herself. I was always impressed by her ability to pay attention to the details. It was also Shannon who one time reminded me as I went to speak to the South Carolina Republican Women's Club that many women love flowers. We stopped by a store and picked up three hundred roses, one for each of the Republican women attending the annual event. Without any question, it was a hit as we passed out a rose to each person in the room.

Needless to say, while I've benefited from legislating with these powerful teammates, perhaps the lasting and enduring value is the friendships that will never fade. We all experienced the changes the country went through from 2008 to 2010, with the election of President Obama and the rise of the Tea Party. As the nation's priorities changed, I began to feel a call to serve in a different way.

SERVING IN A DIFFERENT WAY

While I was working diligently in Columbia, President Obama went to work with a supermajority in both houses of Congress. This allowed him to do what even Bill and Hillary Clinton could not accomplish, passing a massive piece of legislation that would turn over many Americans' health-care decisions to Congress and the federal government. Obamacare, as it became known, served as a rallying cry for conservatives who had had enough. The health-care law would turn over one-eighth of America's economy to elected officials and bureaucrats who had very little working knowledge of one of the most important areas of American life. Two critical parts of Obamacare were the establishment of an Independent Payment Advisory Board that could, in the future, be responsible for health-care rationing decisions, as well as the individual mandate to purchase insurance or pay a penalty. This, I believe, was one of the first times an American would be penalized for *not* doing something, and the courts recently agreed.

The country was changing as President Obama shifted us to the left, and I became more and more focused on those nationwide issues. I was the first member in the state House to introduce a law repealing Obamacare in South Carolina. Then, after I had served one term in the state legislature, our local U.S. congressman, Henry Brown, surprisingly announced he would retire. I had already decided to run for lieutenant governor of South Carolina, had raised quite a bit of money, and was actually leading in the polls. Plus, I believed that I would never leave South Carolina. That had been instilled in me more than twenty years earlier, during one of the first times I went to visit my father. In 1989, I flew to Colorado Springs, Colorado, where he was living, to see my dad and his family, including my brother Earl.

I remember stepping off the airplane in Colorado, and the crisp, cool air overwhelmed me. The beautiful mountain landscape was amazing. Earl and I were driving around town in his black Mitsubishi sports car, going what you might call "a little too fast," and a police officer pulled us over. I was understandably nervous, but Earl was as calm and unassuming as one could be. After an extended conversation, the police officer told us to slow down and have a nice day.

He just . . . walked away? No demeaning words or threats? Just a warning? That would have been a rare experience for me in South Carolina. A strong part of me decided I was moving to Colorado Springs right then and there, no questions asked. I could interact with a police officer like that, *and* it was not one thousand percent humidity? What a refreshing experience. Done and done. I could move there right away and figure out whatever I needed to with my dad later.

However, after much prayer and consideration, it became clear to me that the Lord's plan for me and South Carolina was not finished yet. When I ran for Congress years later, that experience is one of the major reasons I hesitated to leave the state that I love. It was not immediate or sudden, but South Carolina has changed so much in the last twenty-five years, and it has truly been an honor to watch, participate, and live in our great state over that time. It is the only place I ever want to live.

I have always been resistant to leaving South Carolina because of my experience returning home after that trip to Colorado. I knew one of the best ways to make progress happen in the Carolinas was through public service. That's why I was laser focused on becoming governor one day, which of course made a run for lieutenant governor perfectly sensible.

I thought back to when I was in high school, and traveled to Belton–Honea Path, South Carolina, for a student government conference. If you aren't familiar with that area of the state, let's just say a black kid from Charleston knew that wasn't the friendliest place to go at that time. I was placed with a white family, and I did not know what to expect. But they were the kindest, most welcoming family I had ever met. I was not uncomfortable for one second after I got there. I learned that I needed to think deeper about things, and that learning experience was only possible because I grew up in South Carolina. It spoke back to that down payment our ancestors had made so that we all could have a brighter future.

In late summer 2009, I found myself on the campaign trail on Hilton Head Island trying to convince Beaufort County voters that I should be their next lieutenant governor. I had raised hundreds of thousands of dollars and was leading in the polls against two candidates that filed months earlier. As I finished my presentation about the challenges of the federal government, Obamacare, and a number of other national issues, my audience told me that while they might look at me as a potential lieutenant governor, they would definitely vote for me as a member of Congress. My message was connecting to the broader national debate on issues that could imperil our country for generations, including South Carolina.

AN OPEN SEAT IN CONGRESS

One Sunday evening in early January 2010, my campaign manager Joe received a call from United States congressman Henry Brown, announcing his retirement from Congress. Open seats are rare, and this was a red-letter day. Joe was quite excited, and he called me immediately to deliver the breaking news. But, as was usually the case on a Sunday evening, I was at a movie with my mom.

So, he texted me: "Tim, Henry Brown is NOT running for re-election!"

I texted him back: "Thanks." That's it. That did not appease him.

He texted me again, reiterating what he had already told me, but this time he used all caps, the widely recognized texting code for *shouting to get my attention.*

I replied: "I am running for lieutenant governor," as if he didn't know that already since he was managing the race. I really didn't want to talk about it. But Joe knew immediately that this was something to stop and consider. It was an opportunity for me to try to remedy some of the major policy problems that our country was facing. Even though I was running for a state-level office, I was campaigning about our nation's growing spending problem, the debt and deficit, rising regulations that were stopping economic growth, and Obamacare. He reminded me after all, that I was the first state representative in South Carolina to pre-file a bill nulli-fying the Affordable Care Act (ACA) in our state.

But I never felt led to go to Washington. Yes, I enjoyed public service, but I wasn't drawn to our nation's capital. On one hand, it wasn't a surprise to him that I was reluctant to discuss it, particu-larly since I was in the middle of another campaign. I was always one who would finish what I started. After a few more attempts that night, Joe finally gave up trying to discuss it with me.

The following morning, I walked into the building that housed the Allstate agency and the campaign office. Joe was already at his desk, and he followed me right into my office. The fact that I didn't really want to have a conversation about it didn't seem to matter to him. He closed the door and we discussed what it would look like to change races. The shift called for some significant chal-lenges, including how we would need to return all of the money we had raised for the statewide race.

Serving in public office had always been a part-time position for me, both in my thirteen-plus years on county council and my first term in the state House. I ran my insurance business full-time while serving in this capacity, as did all other public servants on the county and state level. The prospect of going to D.C. would change that. Joe was insistent that I stop and consider this, and then he reminded me that I was already discussing the many issues our country was facing, and that I could actually do something about them if I was in Congress.

We left it at that.

Well, at noon that day, Henry Brown had his press conference announcing his retirement, and within minutes my phone blew up! People were telling me that I needed to run. "Get in now." "I'll support you!" "You'll scare off any would-be opponents if you announce early." Many of these calls and texts were coming from people I deeply respected, both in and out of politics, so at that point, I knew I had no choice but to at least give it thoughtful consideration.

Joe did not believe I needed to rush to the decision. He told me that if I ran, I would probably win, which obviously meant I'd be going to Washington. My life would effectively change overnight. I needed to take my time. "If there's anyone who would stand down and not run because you're in the race, you will surely defeat them anyway," he told me.

I took my time over the course of a month. I prayed. And I prayed some more. I talked to friends both in and out of politics. I relied on my family, particularly my mom and my aunt Nita. I met with my pastor, Greg Surratt, for wisdom and advice. I kept returning to the mission I set for my life the night before John Moniz's funeral, that "I would positively affect the lives of a billion people with the message of hope and opportunity."

A position in Congress could certainly help reach that huge number. Democrats had forced through Obamacare, and the national debt was increasing at a staggering rate. Republicans were more energized than they had been in a generation. These were issues I believed would affect the lives of South Carolinians as deeply as anything on the state level. We had to take a stand, no matter how uncomfortable I was with the idea of living in Washington three or four days a week.

A DECISION OF FAITH

The decision to enter the race was a decision of faith. There were very good reasons to continue the run for lieutenant governor, and what seemed like a growing mountain of reasons not to join the race for Congress. But, with encouragement from family, friends, and Joe, I decided to throw my hat in the ring and move forward. We would have to start over, return all the donations we had received, and hope folks chipped in for the congressional campaign, and really hit the ground running. On February 8, 2010, I announced I was running for Congress.

Despite Joe's insistence that I was the favorite, I was taking on huge names in South Carolina politics. Strom Thurmond's son Paul was running, as well as Carroll Campbell III, the son of a popular former governor. I had served with Paul for two years on county council. There were nine candidates, including Paul and Carroll. But just as I learned to trust my instincts when I lost to Robert Ford, I knew I had to trust them here as well. It also helped that the climate in 2010 would lead to legacy candidates being at a disadvantage. However, there was also a larger picture at play than just who I was running against. What I was running against, and for, was history. From our very beginning to the present day, Charleston, and South Carolina as a whole, plays a very complicated role in American history. A famous quote by former South Carolina attorney general James Petigru perhaps sums it up best: "South Carolina is too small for a republic and too large for an insane asylum."

Many people focus on South Carolina's role in the Civil War, but eighty years before that we played a huge role in the Revolutionary War as well. Today, if you drive to the serene beaches of Sullivan's Island, about twenty minutes from downtown Charleston, there is no indication of a battle that raged there in June 1776. If you drive far enough down the island, you will see a series of old bunkers and signs that mark Fort Moultrie, but they certainly do not give the visual spectacle that Gettysburg or Fort Sumter do.

As the British came to attack on June 28, 1776, the fort, then known as Fort Sullivan, was not even completed. Its purpose was to protect Charleston, and it was forced into service earlier than expected. With Americans numbering in the hundreds in place under the command of William Moultrie, the odds were stacked against the revolutionaries. But, "By the end of the day, the British withdrew with 200 dead (compared to 12 Colonists) and five of their nine ships either damaged, severely damaged or grounded."

That battle showed just what was possible for the young Americans. They had protected Charleston, and proven the massive British navy was not invincible. If you did the math on the date, you noticed it was six days before the Declaration of Independence.

More than 240 years later, a bill I wrote passed the United States Senate creating Fort Sumter and Fort Moultrie National Historical Park. As is consistent with our provocative history, Fort Sumter, the birthplace of the Civil War, is clearly visible across Charleston Harbor from Fort Moultrie. A short ferry could take you from where the spirit of the revolution was energized in creating our new country in 1776, to where it was broken apart in 1860.

During the Civil War, 625,000 Americans were killed. That was 2 percent of our entire population. To put that in perspective, 2 percent of our population today is more than six million people, or approximately the entire population of Los Angeles and Houston combined. So many were willing to sacrifice their lives for one thing . . . freedom. And that liberty was about one thing . . . slavery.

Some try to make the case that the Civil War was about other things, like states' rights, or labor, or the economy. But the southern states' economies were driven by agriculture, which was powered by black labor, which was only possible due to slavery. States wanted the right to keep enslaving an entire race of people, and brothers were willing to fight brothers over the freedom of people they never met.

It was the greatest tragedy in American history, but one that was necessary to take the most significant step toward freedom for all. My family was enslaved in South Carolina during the Civil War, and while I certainly grew up in far from ideal conditions economically, it was nothing compared to those generations who perished in rice fields and cotton plantations.

Both Fort Moultrie and Fort Sumter are in the heart of South Carolina's 1st Congressional District. A black person had never represented the district in Congress. It had been two hundred years since it had been represented by John C. Calhoun, a former vice president of the United States who had his own issues with race. Then, add on top of that I was running against the son of Strom Thurmond, a man who certainly evolved over his lifetime but also ran for president as a segregationist, and you might not even be able to write a movie script that covers all those bases.

While racial issues seem to be permanently embedded in our politics, I was confident that the evolution of the southern heart would pit our values and positions against each other, and not color. Proving myself in unfamiliar territory would prove challenging and rewarding. If I were to win against a Thurmond or

Campbell, it would speak volumes about our state's evolution. Voters wanted people who believed in their values representing them, plain and simple.

Eventually, we landed in a runoff against Paul Thurmond. That meant two head-to-head debates. I do not use this word lightly, but I loathe debates. I am not a naturally combative person, and that showed in the first debate. I came out flat, and I did not take advantage of the opportunities before me. Luckily, the second debate was the very next day, and I had quickly learned from my mistakes the night before.

As I mentioned, my campaign was based on very conservative themes and timeless principles, such as limited government, less government spending, lower taxes, and national security. On the back of my campaign brochure I included a Contract with the 1st Congressional District. I urged voters to keep the contract and hold me accountable. The promises included protecting the Constitution, rejecting cap-and-trade emissions, fighting for tax cuts, funding our military, and instituting a moratorium on earmarks.

There were nationwide discussions about the prospect of eliminating earmarks, budget busters snuck into law without thorough review and often as favors. Although they represented only approximately 2 percent of our overall budget, our economy was bleeding. I've always said that there is no silver bullet when it comes to balancing a government budget, whether it be county, state, or federal. This was no different. We were not going to find trillions of dollars sitting around in one place. We would need to find money here and there, cut spending where we could, grow our economy, and become more efficient and find areas of waste, fraud, and abuse.

Earmarks played a large role in our campaign, because in 2010 the South Carolina State Ports Authority was in the beginning stages of dredging the port in Charleston. This was and is a federal project with a federal nexus. It was an important project that needed to be done. The port is responsible for one in every eleven jobs in South Carolina. The port needed to be dredged to fifty-two feet to allow for newer and bigger cargo ships to be able to navigate it. It was a project worthy of support and I indeed supported it. As did Paul Thurmond.

But the question posed to both Paul and me that second night was "Would you, if necessary, earmark the port project if that is what it took to get the project funded?"

Paul said he would do whatever it takes to get the port funded—that's how important this project was to not just the coast but to our entire state. My position was different. I said, "No, I would not."

Earmarks were one of the reasons we were in the mess we were in. The fact that earmarks "only" represented 2 percent of our country's overall spending wasn't the point. We were going further and further into debt every day. Furthermore, President Obama used earmarks to fund several projects that were promised to some members of Congress whom he needed to persuade to support Obamacare.

My position was clear—the Charleston port needed to be dredged. It was a worthy project and worthy projects should get funded—the right way! Not through earmarks, but by winning a competitive bidding process. Our port is important for the nation as a whole, and I knew we would clearly and fairly win through any competitive grant program.

This position was also risky. The district and state were divided on the question. When one in every eleven jobs is tied to a particular project, it's best you weigh that when making decisions. But our country was in trouble. This was bigger than the port. It was bigger than South Carolina and it certainly was bigger than me. Our country needed someone to take a stand.

This position also caught the attention of South Carolina's junior senator, Jim DeMint. Senator DeMint had become a vocal proponent of ridding our country of earmarks. He heard my positions regarding earmarks and the port dredging project, and that Paul saw things differently. Because of this difference between Paul and me, he decided to weigh in on the race. He didn't outright endorse me but provided a quote supporting my position on earmarks. He allowed me to use the quote any way I wanted, so we placed it on a direct mail piece and mailed it to Republican primary voters so they could see the difference between Paul and me regarding this very important fiscal issue.

He didn't need to do this. He was a sitting senator and did not benefit at all by weighing in on a congressional race in the middle of the primary, and oh, by the way, my opponent was Strom Thurmond's son. But he felt the need to take a stand, too.

I cannot overstate how much I supported—and still support—the South Carolina State Ports Authority. But I also support America, and I firmly believed that the project was worthy of funding without needing an earmark to get it done. I was right, and I have no doubt that at least to some degree, this issue was one of the reasons why the margin of victory was as large as it was.

Here it comes again, a statement I make often: thankfully, Joe ran an amazing campaign. Some big names in the Republican Party, Eric Cantor and Kevin McCarthy, had supported me, and I was blessed with a victory. I was most proud that we were able to be sensitive and involved with the voters of Horry County and Georgetown County, who always felt like they were in second place in the district behind Charleston. Historically, most of the congressmen elected in the 1st District were from Charleston, so it was easy to see how they came to that conclusion. Knocking on doors personally in Myrtle Beach would prove helpful as it brought out a "He's For Us" mentality among voters.

Overall, we won 68 percent of the vote, and I was headed to Washington for literally the first time ever. As it turned out, a record-breaking number of Republicans across the country were joining me.

"Far and away the best prize that life has to offer is the chance to work hard at work worth doing."

—THEODORE ROOSEVELT

CHAPTER 10

THE CHALLENGES
OF WASHINGTON

THE CAPITOL HILL CLUB, a Republican respite in the middle of the hustle and bustle of congressional life, is the place where I have dinner with dear friends like Trey Gowdy and John Ratcliff. It's no Chick-Fil-A, but quiet, professional and usually removed from the tensions that fill a normal day at work in the Capitol.

On this evening, back in December of 2017, sitting among the beautiful decorations for the Christmas season, I was as focused and excited as I had been since arriving in Washington as a freshman congressman five years earlier. For months I had worked my heart out on legislation that would become the Tax Cuts and Jobs Act. The bill included major commonsense provisions for families and children, as well as the creation of Opportunity Zones.

But we were in a harsh stalemate in the Senate—one that was a lethal threat to the tax-cut bill. Of course, every Democrat opposed it, and we were struggling to keep the Republicans on board. Most troubling to me was that a pivotal vote was in the hands of one of the people I most admire in Washington—Senator Marco Rubio of Florida.

The source of the stalemate was not complicated. Senator Rubio wanted the child tax credit in the legislation to be higher than the $1,400 now called for in the bill. The highest we had been able to go without losing votes was $1,000. We were in a delicate dance. Yet, Marco was adamant in his sincere belief that the figure should be higher. Otherwise, he would vote "No" which would kill the bill my colleagues and I had worked so hard on.

So, this was the heavy burden on my heart that evening as I joined my friends, Congressmen Gowdy and Ratcliff, for dinner. We talked about all sorts of things, but for me the elephant in the room, as they say, was the situation with Marco. In my pondering, I began glancing around and realized that, thinking of elephants in the room, they were everywhere! Big elephants! Little elephants! Glass elephants! Wooden elephants! Elephants in glass cases! Yep, this was the Republican's Capitol Hill Club, and that means elephants.

At least I could smile.

As we were chatting over dinner, a call came in on my cell phone. It was Senator Rubio. I excused myself and found a quiet place to take the call. I didn't dare let myself think Marco was going to back down on his demand—and, sadly, that was wise on my part. He was as committed as ever to a figure higher than I could negotiate. He believed quite sincerely that setting a higher figure was extremely important in helping young families across America.

When I returned to the table, Trey considered my demeanor and commented that something terrible must have happened. I confirmed his observation, and then we briefly discussed the impasse. I was sure that my months of work on my dream legislation, including Opportunity Zones, was all for naught.

As I do at such times, my thoughts turned to my family and all the struggles of my mother as well as what this legislation would do for millions of single moms like her. I was focused on little else other than what I could do to keep our bill from imploding. The prospects were not promising.

But, of course, an important lesson from my family is that no matter what, you have to get up and keep going and never give up. So, the next day, I went back to my key "Yes" votes among the senators and renewed my arguments for seeing things Senator Rubio's way, urging them to agree to his desire for a higher child tax credit so that we would have the critical 51st vote to pass the legislation.

A day or so later, after fierce arguments with colleagues, we had a breakthrough. I informed Senator Rubio that others had yielded and that the legislation now set the child tax credit at $2,000. (And I was happy to tell him that I personally thought it was a better bill with the increase.) What we had been through, as difficult as it was for all of us, was pretty much the way nearly all significant legislation is usually achieved.

Several days later, the full Senate approved the legislation with a 51-49 vote. A few days after that, on December 22, 2017, President Trump signed our tax cut bill into law.

Immediately afterward, I called my legislative assistant, Shay Hawkins, and my Chief of Staff, Jennifer DeCasper. These are the people who help make sure I can get things done, and they would help me immensely as we implemented our Opportunity Zones program in the months to come. Jennifer, in particular, has become an integral part of my team.

Of course, it didn't start out that way.

BUILDING MY TEAM

Hard as it might be to believe now, Jennifer's interview for her first job on my staff didn't go so well. She didn't answer any questions particularly well; she told me that she had blown the interview *while she was still in the interview*; and she cried. It was a rough start.

Jennifer was a single mom who had just turned her life upside down to come back to Washington because she felt compelled to serve. She couldn't find a legislative job, and was working on the tarmac at Dulles International Airport as one of those ground workers who direct planes to terminal parking slots. Summers in D. C. are already blazing hot, and she was nearly melting on the black tarmac, surrounded by planes blowing hot air out of their jet engines. She was depressed, disappointed, and unsure how this had become her life.

When we met again after her failed interview with my office, Jennifer told me of an incident on the broiling hot tarmac. She found herself thinking out loud, talking at first to herself, and then wondering if she was talking to God. *How did this happen? How is this my life? And is this how someone talks to God?*

Just in case, she asked God to talk back. And in that moment, a butterfly fluttered past. There's not much nature on or near a tarmac. It smells like jet fuel. There's no place where a butterfly could have come from, and there was nowhere for it to land. And yet, there it was, flying extra close to her—even a little too close for comfort. More like an annoying gnat than a charming butterfly. But, Jennifer says, in a strange and comforting way, she began to feel like she wasn't alone after all. Maybe things were really, truly about to change.

When we were first in contact with Jennifer, she was interviewed by Joe and my first chief of staff, Nick Muzin. I'm sure she didn't expect to have another interview the next morning. But, indeed, the very next morning, when we called and asked her to come in for a second interview in a couple of hours, she had to leave her work and run to Target to pick out the right interview clothes. She rushed to get to the office on time to meet with me, so I'm sure she was more than a little flabbergasted.

Yes, she had been very emotional in her second interview, but in the end, that transparency actually showed me her heart. I had prayed to the Lord to send me someone who had not just knowledge, but the heart to help lead our office forward. Here she was, tears and all. I hired Jennifer DeCasper that day in 2010, and a decade later, she's now going into her fourth year as my Senate chief of staff.

After hiring Jennifer and filling out my staff, it was time to get to work. Trey, Mick, Jeff, and I quickly made names for ourselves. We were incredibly vocal about repealing Obamacare and getting our nation's debt under control. President Obama was threatening to raise the debt ceiling by executive order, and there were two budget showdowns in the first eight months of the year. We made national headlines for heading to the House Chapel to pray before one of the votes.

You read that right—it was a story that four Christians prayed before making a huge decision that would affect not just them, but everyone in the country. One upset caller to my office asked how we were any different from the Taliban! I knew how I was going to vote and was simply seeking wisdom through prayer to provide clarity in time where emotions where running high. Some might be confused as to why prayer was needed when I knew what I was going to do, but it makes perfect sense to me. When tensions are high, and there is all sorts of external noise and pressure, prayer can strip away all of those other things and help you refocus on the task at hand.

Some folks portrayed us as crazy (probably because we didn't vote the way they wanted us to), and I still can't believe it. While there were certainly some members of the 2010 class that wanted to burn the house down, that was not us. We were simply conservatives; driven by principles to do what the people of our districts had sent us to Washington to do. Speaker John Boehner was a good man, but he never really grasped that fact, and we didn't always see eye to eye. We weren't there to do things as they had always been done. That attitude earned the four of us a nickname—the Four Horsemen.

THE FOUR HORSEMEN

We voted against the creation of the sequester by the Budget Control Act, which would automatically slash government programs and our military if a long-term budget deal was not reached. This was one of the all-time ill-conceived ideas ever to come out of Congress, and it was doomed to fail from the beginning. Democrats felt under siege after getting blown out in the 2010 elections. Republicans were on a mission to get spending under control, and Democrats kept moving the goalposts.

This deal was a mistake, and we said so. Why weren't we focusing on tax reform? On finding common ground for smart regulations or ways to increase economic growth? Instead we put our military on the chopping block, and it is only just now beginning to recover. I have no doubt the deal was done with good intentions, but sometimes good intentions don't make up for bad ideas.

We saw those bad ideas come to fruition almost immediately. Our cuts to our military gutted the tools and resources necessary to keep our soldiers ready and well trained, and as it began to be implemented, I got up close and personal with just how important it was for us to get it fixed.

One of the positive lasting legacies of my father is his military service and what it did for me as a young man. Even though he was not around, I always had an affinity for the military and those who served our country because of him. I think he is also a significant reason my brothers, Ben and Earl, decided to serve and make the military their career.

In talking with veterans and active-duty members of our armed forces, it is sometimes hard for people to put into words just why they signed up to serve. There are a lot of different reasons, all weighted differently. But one thing they all know is that they are willing to put their lives on the line for our country. They believe that despite what is happening in their own lives—marriage, kids, other possible careers—that fighting for the greater good is worth the stress that it places on all those other things. We are all thankful for our troops and their families every single day, and I am proud that my dad and many others have served their country with distinction.

I knew when I came to Congress that I wanted to leverage my position to honor our veterans—for folks like my dad, who was in Thailand during the Vietnam war just a few months after my mom learned she was pregnant with me, or members of the Greatest Generation who stormed the beaches at Normandy.With the special place the Vietnam War holds in my family, I also knew that so many of them returned to a country weary of war, and one that was not willing to give them the applause and commendation they deserved.

So, in 2012, we started holding Veterans Honor Ceremonies across South Carolina. We started with World War II veterans, and we hoped we could attract around 150 veterans and their families for a special ceremony, and to receive a certificate of appreciation and ceremonial lapel pin. When the day came, we had more than six hundred veterans attend the ceremony. It was a chilly morning, and I was nervous. Honoring these men and women was a huge responsibility, and I knew we had to ensure the ceremony properly respected their legacy. Many were getting fragile in their old age, but the steel in their eyes and strength in their handshake gave a glimpse into the heroism of their younger days.

Pat Waters, General George Patton's grandson, brought his grandfather's boots and placed them on the podium as he gave the keynote speech. Pat did a remarkable job honoring those heroes with whom his grandfather had served. To remember those lost, there was also a stirring rendition of taps, and I can guarantee you there was not a dry eye in the house. We went aisle by aisle, shaking hands with every veteran and honoring every hero by listening to their sacrifices. It was a privilege to honor their sacrifices, to show them their stories matter, even more than fifty years later. They truly saved the world from the horror of Hitler, and so many made the decision to do so at the tender young age of eighteen or nineteen.

When we started planning the World War II event, we hoped to just have a nice turnout, and by the time the ceremony ended we knew it was something we had to continue in the years to come. In 2013, we honored our Korean War veterans with ceremonies in Spartanburg and North Charleston and ended up seeing more than nine hundred folks combined. Then in 2014 came Vietnam, which we knew would be different from the two previous events. First, there are many more Vietnam veterans still with us than World War II and Korea, which meant the ceremony could be significantly larger. Second, the emotions attached to the Vietnam War are so raw for so many, even now, and we knew we had to acknowledge that while honoring these veterans. And finally, my own family's personal history with the Vietnam War added a little extra emotion for me.

We decided to hold the event at First Baptist Church in downtown Columbia, which had a capacity in the thousands and whose central location in the state would give every veteran an equal opportunity to come. The church was pastored at that time by my friend Pastor Wendell Estep, and they were very excited to host.

Every year First Baptist hosted a Fourth of July celebration that was absolutely incredible; they had music, fireworks, flags, and videos to celebrate the freedom we sometimes take for granted. It was quite simply the perfect location for the event. The morning of the ceremony, even though it was overcast and sprinkling rain, there was a buzz just driving up to the church. We had Vietnam military memorabilia outside and in the lobby, and a map of Vietnam for veterans to pin where they had served. People were laughing, talking, and sharing stories, which was quite the juxtaposition to the reception they received on coming home so many years ago. Not all the veterans knew each other, but they knew they were kindred souls because of what they had gone through, both at home and abroad.

Local Boy Scouts were at every entrance to welcome the veterans and their families, to serve food, and to usher people to their seats. We almost filled the church as nearly 2,400 people showed up that day. Our keynote speaker was Major General James E. Livingston, USMC (Ret.), a marine who served in Vietnam and is a recipient of the Medal of Honor due to his heroics there. He noted as he drove that the drizzly morning was "a Vietnam morning," and the crowd loved it. He had served with these guys, and his speech was inspirational.

As always, I spoke as well, and I had to choke back my emotions before I could simply tell those in attendance, thank you. Taps once again moved the entire venue to tears, and at the conclusion of the event, I stayed to meet every single veteran who would give me the honor of shaking their hand. It was ninety minutes before I even took a step.

One veteran approached me with tears in his eyes. He told me he had never been thanked for his service in Vietnam. Not even once. That put a lump in my throat as we talked. It seems like such an easy thing to do to just say "thank you" to someone who had sacrificed his youth and seen so many friends die. He had scars from his time as a soldier, scars that would never go away. Amazingly, he was not alone. Over and over this scene repeated itself, and every single time I felt that same lump in my throat.

You might think something as simple as a certificate and a pin would be discarded by men and women who bled for their country and saw their friends killed and even blown up. Instead, I felt their desire for a public recognition for their service, and they truly deserve it. Those emotions, that feeling, made that two or three hours after the ceremony unlike any other experience I have had with constituents.

I was totally swarmed, and yet I felt totally safe. As a senator, you get used to folks coming up everywhere you go, sometimes friendly, often not. You get used to it, and rarely feel overwhelmed by what is happening around you. It is safe to say at this event, my emotions took over. So many veterans wearing their hats or vests with patches, all gathered with a sense of pride and thanksgiving.

The emotions did not simply come from seeing the memorabilia, or hearing General Livingston's speech, or the map to pin. The certificates didn't do it, nor the Battle Hymn of the Republic. It wasn't the videos we ran before and after, or even when we recited the Pledge of Allegiance and some started to cry.

I pledge allegiance to the flag of the United States of America, and to the Republic for which it stands, one

nation under God, indivisible, with liberty and justice
for all.

We have all heard it before, and these men and women had
more than most. It was just different that morning. So was the
National Anthem, beautifully done, and with hands to hearts and
caps raised quicker than I've ever seen.

It was more than the sum of all that. They knew that, more
than six hundred months later, South Carolina and the nation
had finally come together to say thank you. It was a foreign experience, and the emotional surge they felt was involuntary and
almost like instinct. They were responding to something they
had been hungry for ever since they returned home, and which
we were more than eager to give them that morning.

I carry those feelings with me every single time Congress
works on military and veterans' issues. This is why, as the years
rolled on, the sequester became more and more unacceptable.
We continued with ceremonies for our Desert Storm and Desert
Shield veterans, as well as all our women veterans, and each year
it became more and more urgent to get things fixed. We were
letting our service members fall behind, when we should have
been ensuring they remained the best-equipped and most well-
trained fighting force the world has ever seen. At these events, I
met thousands of veterans, men and women, who had made deep
sacrifices. At a minimum, they gave up multiple years of their
youth, and at worst, they encountered life-changing injuries that
still affect them today.

Worst of all is that the U.S. Department of Veterans Affairs
was in virtual shambles. Why didn't Congress just do our dang
job and make sure we were helping everyone as best we could?
President Trump has restored record-high funding to the mili-

tary, and we have increased funding and services for our veterans and the VA. Furthermore, veterans now have expanded services outside the VA.

DIFFICULT ISSUES

Four years after our Vietnam ceremony, while serving my only year on the Senate Armed Services Committee, I got an up-close and personal look at just how terrible the Budget Control Act (BCA) was. Thankfully, the tide had finally shifted, and I was proud to work on the 2018 National Defense Authorization Act, which finally started putting the pieces back together. But we lost six years because Congress was simply afraid to make a tough choice, one that the class of 2010 had been specifically elected to make. Looking back on how everything happened, it comes back to a larger point that runs throughout our society these days.

Too often, people take too long to admit they made a mistake. We all do it. Heck, the first three decades of my life was a series of learning from my mistakes. But when you're playing with the lives of our troops, veterans, and the American people, it is absolutely unacceptable to do so. The way the sequester was set up, there was a grace period where a special committee was formed to try to find a spending deal where cuts were made based on merit, as opposed to swinging an axe blindly at everything.

This special committee was called the Supercommittee, and I knew it was destined to fail, which played into my voting no on the BCA. But if things had gone differently and it worked, I would have been the first to celebrate any progress we made. They had four months to find $1.2 trillion in budget reductions, and it went absolutely nowhere. How on earth, then, did it take Congress almost a decade to admit that passing the sequester did nothing to actually solve our spending and debt issues, and only hurt our troops and good programs?

That was one of many questions we had to stare down almost immediately upon coming to Congress. When you arrive in D.C., there is an explosion of new policy issues and the knowledge base you have to build on them. And in our nation, seemingly no matter what the news of the day or the legislative battle for six months is, the issue of immigration is always lurking in the background. In my opinion, there is no issue more complex, life-altering, and hotly debated than immigration.

We have been searching for an answer for decades, especially after the well-intentioned but failed 1986 immigration reform package. The most amazing component of this issue is that arguments arise from so many different angles—some are statistical, others purely from the heart, nonborder states versus border states, and those who teeter and step over the line of simply hyperbolic, unnecessary, and insensitive language.

I believe we have to understand that part of the American story is not just "send us your tired, your poor, your huddled masses," but also the willingness of those looking to come here to become part of the fabric of this nation. The process of illegally entering our nation only makes it harder for the immigrant and our nation as a whole to find that balance. We must find a system that aligns with our values and what is in our heart, while encouraging that acclimation that binds us together.

I am passionate about this issue both because I believe the greatness of America includes welcoming those who want to come here the right way, and because I have seen it done firsthand.

After my brother, Ben, enlisted in the Army, he was stationed in a few different spots around the world. After a few years, while he was stationed in South Korea, he called me one day to tell me he had met a beautiful woman and was going to marry her. I was very happy for him, and after congratulating him, I asked where she was from. Ben told me plainly that she was from "around here." Oh great, I responded, so is she from Summerville or Goose Creek? Ben let me know that while Mia was from the south, it was not South Carolina but South Korea.

When it was time for them to come home to America, it was clear Ben's wife wanted to immigrate here through the front door. She did not speak much English, but she was determined to become an American citizen. It took her seven years, but she finally did. And along the way, she gave us all the best present we have ever gotten—my nephew Ben, the heir to the Scott Throne, as I call him.

Mia recognized that part of coming to the United States was embracing what it meant to be an American. That did not mean she stopped loving her family back in South Korea, or any of the people with whom she grew up. It reinforced her knowledge that culturally acclimating to America was as important as physically coming here in the first place.

WE MUST GET IT RIGHT

When we speak of the American melting pot, we are in part talking about that process of becoming an American. There is an American standard, and it is hard to reach that if you are not willing to part with your past to move forward in this great nation. It requires embracing a new ethos and leaving the previous one behind. Illegal immigration encourages separation and a lack of integration into our society as a whole. That, more than any political debate, is why we have to tackle the issue. There are tens of millions of people in this country who are first- or second-generation Americans, and some estimates show that 1 in 15 immigrants worldwide are coming to the United States. We are a shining light, and people are not going to stop wanting to come here. That is why we have to get this right.

There is no doubt that today, the issue of illegal immigration feels different than it has in the past. Why has illegal immigration at our southern border stoked so many fires across the country, turning folks against each other even at game night or at the dining room table? I think it would be easy to blame the internet, or cable news, and there is certainly some validity there. But hunkering down to a diet of rumor-mongering and engaging false reporting seems to have become the comfort zone for too many.

I think it goes deeper than that, though. There is an anger and in some ways a lack of understanding as to how this nation was built. Make no mistake, we are a nation of laws, and those laws must be enforced. I do not condone or excuse illegal immigration. We must create a merit-based system and reject the notion that immigration issues boil down to race.

I support the building of a wall, but it's not a silver bullet. Put a wall up, people will dig under it. Shut the tunnels down, people will sail around them. We must have a holistic approach to solve illegal immigration, and it must be a multipronged approach, undertaken with the knowledge that as long as we are the greatest nation on the planet, some will do whatever they can to bring their families here.

Said another way, a major part of the problem with fixing our immigration system is just how complex the issue has become. The political angle alone creates all sorts of pressure on both sides. One creative approach has been a partnership at Mexico's southern border, but the Democrats know that the longer they hold the issue hostage, the better it is for them as an election issue. There is no pressure for them to actually solve the problem when they can continue to paint Republicans as heartless racists. The fact that they allow this to continue, when they know full well a compromise can be found, is antithetical to how a good government should operate. In other words, the Democrats would rather talk about this issue than actually solve it.

As for Republicans, too often we allow the worst possible spokespeople for our party to be heard. Painting with a very broad brush, we should do much better with the Hispanic population than we do. A high percentage are Catholics with conservative social values, and polling shows that tough immigration policies are not deal breakers for many. "Specifically, most Latinos who were born abroad say they are worried about deportations, but the majority of Latinos who were born in the United States are not."

Putting aside the political problems, this is really an issue of who we want to be as a nation. I am not, nor would I ever, ask someone to deny their family or forget their heritage. What makes every individual unique in their own way is the same quality that can contribute to creating a stronger United States of America. We are absolutely, positively better together.

But people must also want to do things the right way. Breaking in through the back door is not something we can or should tolerate. There is not a nation on earth as welcoming as we are, but we still have laws that must be upheld. That, more than anything, is why when tackling immigration, we have to start at the border.

It is not fair to people like my sister-in-law, Mia, who came here the right way, worked hard, and earned her citizenship, for us to fail in finding a solution. America is the land of opportunity, not one where we should reward short-circuiting the process. We have big hearts, open arms, and the knowledge that our laws are on the books for a reason.

Knowing all of this, thinking through it, and trying to deter-

mine my position on the intricacies of immigration was just one of
the many issues I had to sort through when running for Congress.
Do not get me wrong, I would not trade it for the world, but you
learn very quickly on a federal campaign just how big and tough
some of these issues truly are.

While we were fighting these policy battles, my staff and I
also were given a clear look at the culture war being waged at
the same time. It was also during the time around the Budget
Control Act that my office had to shut the phones down because
of an onslaught of racist calls opposed to my vote. "I'll never drive
through your N state again," they said, and "tell that N boss of yours
to get his head out of his $%^&." Calls like these drove our staff and
interns to tears. These weren't from people in South Carolina, but
New Jersey, Illinois, California, and so many other states.

While I had become immune to situations like these occurring
throughout my life, the shock on my staff's faces told a different
story. We had a diverse staff both ethnically and geographically,
with Hispanics, Asians, blacks, and whites coming from South
Carolina, California, Texas, Georgia, Colorado, and more. And
yet, they were all overcome with emotion when this happened.

We were used to nasty letters and angry phone calls. But
purposefully calling a member of Congress you disagree with
simply to hurl racial epithets? Some folks were so creative with
their language and insults I had to explain what a few of them
meant to a couple of staffers. As a boss, and a human, that is not
a conversation you ever hope to have. I think it opened a lot of
people's eyes not just inside the office, but outside as well. Telling other members or staffers what had happened, on both sides
of the aisle, the resounding reactions were shock and sadness.

This would happen a few more times over the years, and given
how quickly staff changes on Capitol Hill, there were always a

few folks in the office who had not experienced it. Every single time the reaction was the same, no matter the staffer's race or where they were from. If a black man could not escape that sort of racism as a United States senator, where could they? I even had one staffer, whom I respect quite a bit, confide that before working for me, racism was an abstract concept, something brushed off as a myth. Now that person is telling people just how real both are, and how important it is that we listen to folks from all parts of the spectrum.

I guess that was a rather long way of saying it, but I am so thankful for my staff, how they devote so much of themselves to our goals, and how they continue to grow, not just as professionals but as people. We have one of, if not the most, diverse staffs on the Hill, and that exchange of ideas involving people from all different backgrounds has been absolutely critical. I have been lucky to have strong and intelligent women lead my office, as well as folks from almost every ethnic background you can imagine. We have even had other offices, both Republican and Democrat, ask for advice as to how they could expand their own offices' diversity.

Diversity does not mean intentionally going and finding someone to check a box. It means widening your view of where qualified candidates come from and making sure everyone has the opportunity to show what they can do. It is no secret that Capitol Hill hires from a very insulated group of people, and so we have worked hard to burst that bubble. As an example, we've formed partnerships with historically black colleges and universities and a variety of different organizations, and we make sure that students all across South Carolina hear about our internship programs.

The diversity of our staff helps me serve America better. Having people from different racial backgrounds is important, but

I am also so thankful to serve alongside staff members with intellectual and physical disabilities. We have partnered with George Mason University in Virginia, which has a program specifically built to help students with disabilities gain work experience and employment. That has shown me that these awesome students are without a doubt people first, and their unique traits help make them amazing people. We have had staffers with autism and bipolar disorder, as well as physically paralyzed. Watching our staffers with intellectual disabilities grow and expand their horizons has been one of the most meaningful experiences during my time in office, and it shows again just how much stronger we can be when we accept all people as they are, and work toward a common goal together.

That sort of bond helped us stay focused after that first explosion of ringing racism during the Budget Control Act vote. We were able to continue chugging along and begin developing the foundations of what would become my Opportunity Agenda. I like to say now that even though I am Senate made, I was House broken. It was here that my long-term staff and I began to learn how to put the lessons I have learned in my life into policy goals and reaching those one billion people with a message of hope and opportunity.

We knew that staying personally connected to the people of the 1st District was key; you would never read a story about me spending too much time in Washington. We started a series of events we called "Talkin' Shop with Tim," where I would work at different businesses around town and invite our wonderful neighbors throughout the 1st District to both share their thoughts and concerns with me, and have me literally serve them.

I pumped gas and cleaned windshields at an Exxon station in West Ashley, harking back to my first job as a thirteen-year-old.

In perhaps the biggest risk a restaurant owner has ever taken, I waited tables at my favorite restaurant, California Dreamin', one afternoon. I helped deliver UPS packages for a day, leading to an onslaught of "what can brown do for you" jokes. I even checked shoppers out at the Piggly Wiggly in Moncks Corner, testing my ability to bag groceries without them spilling all over the floor.

Perhaps the most amazing thing about all of these different ideas was to see the shocked faces when folks realized they were talking to their Congressman. It does not seem so weird to purposefully go out into the community to serve and talk with your constituents, instead of just hitting the normal luncheon circuit and calling it a day. It reinforced that the more comfortable people are with not just you as a person, but their surroundings as well, the more likely you are to get the unvarnished truth from people. Sometimes the stories were hard to hear, but I appreciated that I had earned the opportunity to hear it.

We also put together a day-long "Regulations Tour," where we visited local businesses to help highlight how government red tape was affecting business owners and customers in ways you would never consider. There were Dodd-Frank regulations making it harder for home builders to gain access to capital, and therefore not able to complete homes in booming communities, or trucking regulations that threatened both jobs and the costs of goods. We even discovered that catch limits placed on fishermen by the National Oceanic and Atmospheric Administration, or NOAA, were based on decades-old science and inconclusive data while threatening to put small fishermen out of business.

Taking the lessons we learned from my home district, my staff and I hustled all throughout the second half of 2011 and 2012 with an important goal in mind—receiving a prize spot on the House Ways and Means Committee, which has jurisdiction over the tax code and any tax reform efforts. For a guy whose first bill introduced in Congress was a bill to cut taxes, this was a big deal.

I had a ton of ideas for how we could move forward on House Ways and Means. With Barack Obama as president, they probably would not go anywhere for a while, but the old wisdom is that it takes ten years to get a new idea passed through Congress. So, whatever we could start doing now would pave the way for the future.

There is an old cliché in politics that says, "It's not your seat until you win reelection." Knowing that this is true, it was interesting that my first reelect was in a newly drawn 1st Congressional District in South Carolina. The original 1st District included Horry County, and I gave that up in order to pick up Beaufort County, which consists of Hilton Head Island, Beaufort, and Bluffton.

As you know, the census occurs every ten years, and population shifts also shift congressional districts. South Carolina's population has grown to the extent to which we garnered our 7th Congressional District. This affected all six of the current congressional districts.

After winning in 2010, I needed to yet again present myself to a new voting bloc in Beaufort County for the 2012 election. Then, two phone calls from two old friends changed everything.

"America is another name

for opportunity."

—RALPH WALDO EMERSON

CHAPTER 11

#SENATE

AFTER I APPEARED beside President Trump at the signing ceremony for the new tax reform bill, someone on Twitter (who has since deleted his account) called me, in a series of angry tweets, a "prop" and a "house n****r." Now, I'm not one to get worked up over things, but I couldn't let this one slide. Not only was this person referring to me with a vicious racial slur, but he hadn't even been accurate while doing it.

I decided to come back at him with a single word.

#Senate.

That was my way of doing a couple of things. One, I wasn't in the House anymore, I was in the Senate. But second, it was also to dismiss his nonsense.

When the Senate set its eyes on cutting taxes for the first time in thirty years, we were serious. Senator Orrin Hatch, who was in the Senate in 1986, the last time tax reform was done, called me and said he wanted me to be one of three to focus our efforts on the individual side of the tax code. He and I had several conversations about the importance of cutting taxes on American families.

Did he do so because I'm black? Of course not. He did this because he knew I would bring value to the process.

In this book, you have read that I have always loved and been good with numbers. I had been an elected official for years when we tackled tax reform in 2017. Keeping taxes low has *always* been a priority of mine. When I served on county council, in the state House, and during my one term in the House and in the Senate, a pillar of my campaign platform was to reduce taxes. I've mentioned here that the first bill I filed as a congressman was a bill to lower taxes. So, when the guy who sent the tweet suggested that I was there simply as a prop, why did he think that?

I don't talk about this much, nor do I consider myself a wonk, but I know the budget quite well. To suggest otherwise is disingenuous at best. But before this, I had to become a senator.

BECOMING A SENATOR

On a normal December day in 2012, my life changed forever. I had just won reelection in a newly redrawn 1st District. We spent a lot of time in Beaufort County (which includes Hilton Head Island and Marine Corps Recruit Depot, Parris Island) to meet our new constituents, and we were preparing priorities for the House Ways and Means Committee.

That morning, our office in the Longworth Building was a mess. As I had been in Congress for a full term, I now had the chance to move to a larger office in the Cannon Building. There were boxes and bubble wrap everywhere. There is no packing service in Congress. You pack all your stuff up yourself, and you simply pray you did it well enough so nothing gets broken.

Then, United States senator Jim DeMint called. Jim was the junior senator from South Carolina, and he was well known as a fire-breathing conservative. Some called him the Godfather of the Tea Party, and he certainly earned his stripes fighting for his beliefs and principles. I also knew, in his heart, he was a soft-spoken family man, simply trying to do what he thought was best for the future of the nation.

I knew something was up when his name flashed on my phone screen. While we were certainly friendly, I wouldn't say we called each other often. I went into my personal office in the Longworth Building and closed the door. Jim told me he was preparing to leave the Senate in January 2013, four years before his term was scheduled to conclude. He was leaving to lead the Heritage Foundation, a well-known conservative think tank.

"Shocked" wouldn't be a strong enough word for my reaction. Jim was someone who seemingly reveled in his ability to force the Senate to the right, to cause equal consternation among Democrats and Republicans, and who was uniquely suited for that role. While others like my friend Dr. Tom Coburn had rattled the cages before, no one did it quite like Jim.

I told Joe, Jennifer, and my communications director Sean pretty quickly afterward. We all knew speculation would ramp up immediately about who would fill the seat, and it certainly did. South Carolina law provides that when a U.S. senator does not finish their elected term, the governor appoints a successor to serve until the next statewide election. At that point, an election would occur to finish however much of the term was left. I had served in the South Carolina House with Governor Haley, so we knew each other. However, I really had no clue what was going to happen, because while we were cordial, I would not say we were friends at that point.

Immediately members of the delegation started calling each other to see what we had heard. My answer was true and perplexing—not a thing, not a peep, not a single call from a single person on the governor's team. Joe, who has a great relationship with the entire delegation, started receiving texts from members several times a day. Everyone assumed that we must have known something, anything. The truth is, we literally didn't hear a word from the governor's team for eight days.

It is important to note that Senate seats are incredibly hard to come by, and rarely is there an open seat. South Carolina's former "junior" senator Fritz Hollings was the junior senator for almost forty years. In other words, Strom Thurmond was the senior senator for almost fifty years! You can not only have a birthday waiting for a Senate seat to come open, you can literally grow old waiting for someone to move on from one. The good news for whoever comes next is that I am a believer in term limits!

Every day for the next week, I answered relentless questions about what we knew. The funny thing was, we actually didn't know anything. Short lists were reported, but it's not like Nikki was texting me updates. She knew this was an important decision not just for the person who would become senator, but for her legacy as governor and that of the state of South Carolina as well.

There were so many qualified candidates, led by our entire congressional delegation, former first lady Jenny Sanford and Henry McMaster, to name just a few. I knew I had to just slow everything down, and tell myself that no matter what happened, the people of the 1st District had reelected me to represent them. That was my job. Prognosticating was not going to get me anywhere except a room full of anxiety.

One day as we were waiting to hear some news, Trey Gowdy told me (or in other words, he did not ask me) that he was bringing a *New York Times* reporter named Jennifer Steinhauer to my office. He thought it would be helpful for us to sit down and do an interview on the empty seat. It was one of the first long interviews I had done with a paper the size of the *Times*, so of course I started by thanking Trey for the advance warning.

As we sat down in my office and started talking, we made one thing clear to Jennifer: both of us would be absolutely thrilled if the other was named senator. She wrote, "The two men cannot stop bantering—citing Bible verses, planning lunch, talking about legislation, the wisdom of law school versus no law school (Mr. Gowdy is a former prosecutor, Mr. Scott sold insurance) and debating which of them is more awesome."

Amazingly, being put in front of a national reporter actually helped me relax about the entire process. If it happened, it happened. I had already made a fantastic friend in Trey, and our relationship will last a lifetime, which my days in the Senate surely will not.

After that revelation, it became a little easier to go on as normal as we could while waiting for the governor's decision. I had lunch and saw a movie with my mom in Charleston. My staff went to organizing meetings for House Ways and Means. They told me about all the jokes they heard asking why they were even coming to House Ways and Means when we would just be moving across the Capitol shortly. All this occurred while Governor Haley ruminated for three, four, five . . . seven days. I nervously awaited the governor's decision for a job I was not 100 percent sure I wanted.

Then the tragedy at Sandy Hook Elementary School in Newtown, Connecticut, happened on December 14. This stopped everything, everywhere. How could someone do such a thing? How would this town, these parents put their lives back together? And what, if anything, could Congress have done to stop it?

This really put everything in perspective. Here I was trying to just do my job with rumors running around 24/7 about me becoming a senator, and twenty six- and seven-year-old kids were murdered in their school along with many of their teachers. I'll never forget those feelings. My predicament no longer seemed important.

The next day, I received a call from Jon Lerner, who worked closely with Governor Haley at the time and still does to this day. He relayed a message from the governor that she "may" want to touch base with me on Sunday. Jon didn't tell me if I was the only person she wanted to interview or discuss the possible appointment with, or if she was calling to tell me she had considered me, but it was a no-go. I was clueless, but now even more anxious.

Sunday, December 16, was Joe's niece Kirsten's wedding. I have known Kirsten since she was born, so I was very excited for her that day. I must concede that I was a tad distracted at the wedding, but she was a beautiful bride. Earlier that day, the governor's office called and invited me to the governor's mansion for a discussion with the governor around six or seven o'clock that evening. So, while I'm sure I was enjoying the wedding, I don't remember a single thing about the reception.

My mind was running through every conceivable outcome and question that might come up at the mansion. It had been almost nine days since Senator Jim DeMint had announced his resignation, and I was still in the dark about who the actual potential replacements might be. I got in my car and left the reception after about thirty minutes. I was able to hug the bride and groom and rush to my car to see what was on the governor's mind! I drove to Columbia, about one hundred miles from Charleston, quickly without speeding. Okay, maybe a little faster than the speed limit, but certainly within 5 miles per hour of the limit. I once again ran through every possible scenario, and I tried to be prepared for either outcome.

I called Trey Gowdy on the way to the mansion, and he mentioned that he had a conversation with Nikki as well. He could not tell me anything, though. After I arrived in Columbia, Nikki, her husband Michael, and I spoke for about ninety minutes. She posed questions about our state, the important role we have played, and the role we would continue to play in the nation's success. I shared with her my passion and my journey to Congress. She was, of course, gracious as usual, but also posed questions with her typical frankness.

At the end of our discussion, she asked a simple question. "Tim, would you like to be a United States senator?"

My answer was quick. I said, "Let me pray about it, and I'll call you next week sometime."

Ha! Of course, that's not what I told her! Obviously I had already prayed about it, and my constant prayer had been "God, let Your will be done."

What actually occurred when she asked me that question? I quickly responded with an emphatic yes! With one word, my life and direction took on new meaning, and in an instant my mission of positively affecting the lives of a billion people took a leap forward.

MY MOTHER'S DREAM

My first call was to my mom. It was hard to contain my excitement, but I didn't want to gush. As excited as I was to become a senator, I was more excited about the thought of my mom hearing her son would be the next United States senator for South Carolina. My journey of living her American Dream had taken us somewhere I had never considered even five years before. When we imagine what is possible in this nation, this was a moment that could be written into textbooks. That is not to puff my own chest out, but rather to express my amazement and never-ending thankfulness to be born in a nation where someone who grew up like I did could grow up to become a senator.

When my mom picked up the phone I said, "Mom, are you sitting down?"

She said, "No, I'm washing clothes."

I said, "Well, stop and take a seat!"

She is not accustomed to taking orders from her son, but with a slight sound of irritation, she acquiesced. I told her I had met with the governor, she asked me if I wanted to be a United States senator, and I had said yes.

My mom's response was priceless: she screamed, and she thanked Jesus a lot. I explained to her I had already thanked him so she could stop, but she could not be stopped. My mom continued thanking the Lord. I could no longer hold in my excitement, and I joined her in a hallelujah praise! I am pretty sure the cars next to me on Interstate 26 could hear us.

My mom had worked double shifts, and both her sons turned out to be productive people in society, which was a thrill for her. This proved that all her struggles, pain, and hard work were leading to something bigger. I am forever grateful for the opportunity bestowed, but I am even more elated that my mom and my granddaddy were alive and healthy enough to see the materialization of their blood, sweat, tears, and prayers. So many before me had died to make this possible, from the first slaves in my own family brought to South Carolina in 1815, to the Freedom Riders of the 1960s. Both my mom and granddaddy had lived lives that made this opportunity a reality for me and, more important, for my family.

MOVING FORWARD

Nikki told me we would have a press conference the next morning. Driving back to Charleston, and then back to Columbia the next day, would be a worthwhile journey. It was nearly 9:30 p.m. when I left the governor, and I was still ecstatic and in a state of shock. After I called my mom, I called Joe to share with him that our travel plans for the next day might need to be altered.

Joe answered the phone on the first ring, as if with anticipation of something good about to happen. I said, "Joe, I know we are supposed to fly to Washington tomorrow, but would you rather drive to Columbia instead?"

And he said, "Oh my God! Are you saying what I think you are saying?"

Before I had a chance to answer, he said my name. "Timothy, you got to be kidding me!"

I said, "Nope."

With that one question, his world would change as much as mine.

Joe had been along the journey the entire time. He ran my first race and subsequently every other successful campaign over the next twenty years or so. Joe had forgone his own political ambitions as he had also been a member of the town council of Mount Pleasant and a Charleston County Council member. We were business partners at Allstate and Pathway Realty, and he was my chief of staff in the House. Joe was without a doubt the most consistent and important key to my political success.

Along with the call to Joe, I called my longtime friend Roger. He too had been there all along. Now, nearly thirty-five years after Roger had gotten me that life-changing job at the movie theater, he would stand with me as we embarked on another journey together. It's one of the greatest blessings of life to accomplish things with your lifelong friends, who made the experience and opportunity possible, by your side. Talking to Roger on Sunday evening was like talking to someone in a state of shock. He would later tell me that for the hour after we hung up, he was unmovable. He could not believe it! "This," he said, "is actually going to happen. It's actually going to happen!"

Even more amazingly, Roger had predicted all this happening. Back in 2009, Joe Stringer, whom I worked with at my first insurance agency, Triest & Sholk, was working on a book he was writing. Roger's brother Neil, a pastor on Hilton Head, was visiting for the weekend, and they were having lunch at Michelangelo's. They were talking about getting me in the Senate! It indeed seemed a crazy dream at that point in time.

Joe Stringer came over to the table and asked what they were talking about, and Roger said they were discussing how to ensure Tim becomes a senator. Joe replied that there would not be a state senate seat open anytime soon, to which Roger explained they were talking about the United States Senate. Stringer, who I'm sure thought they were off their rockers, was not sure what to say and just walked away.

When Roger found himself in a state of shock on the night we found out I would become a senator, he immediately thought of that conversation nearly five years earlier. After talking with Joe, Roger, and Trey, who had advocated for me instead of himself, I called my aunt and two more friends. Safe to say I spent the whole drive home on the phone, and I somehow had to figure out how to get to sleep that night.

The next day was a blur. I woke up and tried to follow my routine as best as possible, reading the Bible and listening to worship music. I was in a very reflective mood, and I was thrilled to have my family there with me. My mom, my aunt Nita, my friends Otis, Roger, Joe, Brian Goff, and Michael Sally met at my house to make the drive. When my mom pulled up to the house, she laid on the horn. For a long time. A suspiciously long time. I thought, This was supposed to be a secret, Mom! Be quiet before the neighbors figure out what's going on!

But then it occurred to me: whatever elation I was feeling, she must be feeling tenfold. All the ups and downs of my life, the mistakes I made and the hard work I put in under her watchful eye, they had led to this moment. At my nephew Ben's graduation from both Georgia Tech and Duke, I would have given that horn all it could handle, so I started to understand a little bit.

Once we got to Columbia, there were lights, cameras, and interviews everywhere. While news had begun to leak out in earnest a couple of hours before, Governor Haley's staff did an amazing job of keeping things quiet. We had interviews set up with a Fox News show, as well as a leading conservative website, and that took up a good chunk of time that morning. All the while, I was thinking about what I would say when I walked up to the podium. I was just a kid from North Charleston becoming a senator.

I appreciated that Governor Haley made it a point to directly rebut some of the rumors that I was picked simply because of the color of my skin. "It is important to me, as a minority female, that Congressman Scott earned this seat. He earned this seat for the person that he is. He earned this seat with the results he has shown." In a way, it was almost amusing. After all the challenges I faced because I am black, people were saying I would receive a *promotion* because I am black!

The time came to walk out for the press conference, and almost the entire South Carolina congressional delegation was there. That meant a lot to me, as they are all busy members in their own right. As the press conference began, I realized that it was the largest group of reporters that I had ever seen. Reporters from across South Carolina, Washington, D.C., New York—you name it, they were there. It was truly a scene out of a movie. Governor Haley welcomed me as the next United States senator from South Carolina, and I immediately felt all the light shining directly on me. I heard every flash of every camera. I felt the return of the butterflies that I had felt at Boys' State, before the Charleston Republican Party, when I wanted to run for county council, and so many other important moments of my life. As I continue to do today, I used levity to break the ice. I talked about my mom using the switch, the southern apparatus of encouragement. "I am thankful for a strong mom that understood that love sometimes comes at the end of a switch," I said, "and she loved me a lot."

Funnily enough, talking about receiving the switch from my belt to my ankles got a good chuckle in the room, and I was much more comfortable after that. I thanked my mom and my friends who had helped me get so far. I pledged to continue sticking to my principles, saying, "Our nation finds itself in a situation where we need some backbone. We need to make very difficult decisions." That, of course, still remains true today on everything from fiscal issues to relieving the rising tensions between different factions across the country.

As I look back on it today, it still makes me smile to recall some of the tremendously kind things my colleagues said about me that day. Senator DeMint said, "I can walk away from the Senate knowing that someone is in this seat that is better than I am, that will carry the voice of opportunity conservatism to the whole country in a way that I couldn't do."

Senator Lindsey Graham shared that he thought this moment was long in the making, and even Congressman Jim Clyburn, a

South Carolina Democrat whom I rarely see eye to eye with on policy, said, "The historic nature of this appointment is not lost on me, and I am confident Tim Scott will represent South Carolina and the country honorably."

I had been surrounded by friends and family that day, and it dawned on me just how tough it would be leaving my friends in the House. But I was hopeful to forge new relationships in the Senate. As the only black member of the Senate upon taking office, I found myself again in a historic place.

I really began to lean on Trey Gowdy to help me navigate what was important and what wasn't. I knew Trey and I were, as the kids say, ride or die, so I had someone I could trust who really understood the responsibilities of serving in Congress. That was invaluable and continues to be to this day.

One of the biggest surprises was that my friendship with Trey became an even more important part of my transition to the Senate. As a former prosecutor, Trey's understanding of the legal process would prove helpful in increasing my knowledge of what a good judicial nominee looks like, from their background and temperament to their legal knowledge and application of the law. My staff was certainly good but having a great relationship with Trey meant firsthand knowledge from an undefeated prosecutor who had tried over one hundred cases without a single defeat. This made my job of choosing judges easier and more effective.

Our dinners became more frequent and the company smaller. It's as if the new role gave my friendship with Trey more focus, and the responsibilities before me in the Senate made our journey together more fruitful. Perhaps the most important aspect of our improved relationship wasn't the professional input, but rather the personal distraction from the job of senator and congressman. We came to enjoy talking about anything other than work.

Trey has never been much on politics, as evidenced by the fact that he did not seek reelection in a district that both loves him and misses him. His time in the House was about public service, and he enjoyed taking care of his constituents, and of course cross-examining witnesses before one of his committees. But at dinner he was the funniest guy at the table and would entertain each of our infrequent guests if they didn't mind being the victim of the roast!

While Trey's counsel was certainly invaluable, I was also tasked with growing our staff from fifteen to forty, and quickly. I would now represent forty-six counties instead of just five. I had many new friends, and we had a lot of folks looking for jobs. This would prove to be a team effort on the part of my congressional leaders on the team already. Joe and Jennifer would interview many folks on Senator DeMint's staff, as well as others from around the state looking to join our team. We essentially merged parts of the DeMint staff with our existing staff, as well as some new blood. In Washington, we kept only two of his staffers, and they had both moved on within six months. We did, however, keep some of his state staff, and they have proven indispensable.

I wish I had a grand pronunciation about what my jump from the House to the Senate meant, but to me it really just comes down to God's plan. During the press conference, Joe described me as "very still." I knew this was bigger than me. I was humbled by the task God had now given me, and I was ready for the challenge.

Many of my colleagues expected me to be a firebrand like Senator DeMint. However, they did not have the benefit of knowing the advice that Jim himself gave to me after I was appointed.

Jim told me, point blank, "Do not serve the way I did." He said he had developed his style for a specific plan he felt called to execute. He was a disrupter, and he knew that my outlook on things was different. Jim encouraged me to simply be myself, and to serve in a way that would make me proud of how I did the job.

Finding that style was only the beginning. From growing our staff, to adjusting to life in the Senate, it was clear there was a whole new universe of responsibilities on our plates. I now represented an entire state, and as the dust was settling, those new transitions would make our early decisions pale in comparison.

"It is possible to become discouraged about the injustice we see everywhere. But God did not promise us that the world would be humane and just. He gives us the gift of life and allows us to choose the way we will use our limited time on earth. It is an awesome opportunity."

—CESAR CHAVEZ

CHAPTER 12

THE DARKEST HOUR

FROM MY TIME as a kid on the Air Force base, I had grown up with such an amazing collection of people, and it was an honor to be sworn in to the Senate in January 2013 with so many family and friends around me. Everyone who came that day was my family, including Roger, Joe, Otis, Al Jenkins, my old prayer partner Brandt, and of course my mother, brother, sister-in-law, Aunt Nita, and Clyde. My story had once again come back to my foundation; America has developed as a patchwork quilt with many different people and stories sewn together as one.

Throughout my adult life, I have benefited from a wide array of thinkers. My American story is a story that is inclusive of the diversity of this country, and I am the beneficiary of having learned from many different people what it means to be an American. After becoming the United States senator from South Carolina, the plan was for my first two years in this new position to be rather quiet. In November 2014, I would have to run to complete the last two years of Senator DeMint's term, giving me about twenty-two months to figure out how to best do the job. I learned both

how to represent an entire state, as well as how to navigate the
sometimes odd but always present traditions of the United States
Senate. I was also able to show some of the most decorated leaders of our nation that when we met to discuss important issues,
I take my shoes off. What can I say? I think better that way. That
got more than one odd look, but hey, the truth is the truth.

WORKING UNDERCOVER

My team and I buckled down and introduced my Opportunity
Agenda, my legislative platform to help every American family
have the chance to succeed. We focused on education, workforce development, and job creation. I have long believed in the
great American tapestry, success stitched together with all different colors and types of people. My Opportunity Agenda was our
attempt to reinforce that tapestry, and to ensure that your zip
code, or who your parents were, was not going to determine where
you could end up in life.

Unfortunately, Harry Reid basically shut the Senate down
these two years, as he was not interested in working with Republicans on either side of the Capitol. I am certain we had multiple
bills that would have garnered bipartisan support on the Senate
floor, but they were doomed to never see the light of day. Politics won out over accomplishing objectives to help the American people, and we absolutely need to be better than that. After
the 2012 election, one of the new senators relayed a conversation
with then–majority leader Reid about making progress in the
Senate. The new senator was excited about working in a bipartisan fashion to address some of the challenges he heard about on
the campaign trail. Leader Reid responded that the new senator need not worry about getting things done because he (Reid)
was going to keep the legislative calendar pretty light. He did

not want to jeopardize his majority with tough votes for some of his colleagues. This approach would ultimately backfire as the Democrats lost the majority in 2014.

As part of that process, I knew I needed to hear unvarnished and unbiased opinions from the people of South Carolina. To help learn more about how we could help families from Charleston to Greenville and beyond, I decided to expand on our earlier "Talkin' Shop with Tim" stops, where I had worked as a waiter, checkout clerk at the grocery store and more. I was enjoying watching the show *Undercover Boss,* and I decided that I should begin to go "undercover" in multiple places across South Carolina, working everyday jobs without telling folks who I was. My staff, as most staffs would have been, were not initially thrilled with my decision. I understand why; staff likes to have some level of certainty and control over where they send their boss and how an event is going to turn out. But when I took a few hours one day and simply rode the public bus all around Charleston, I learned as much as I would have in a week of scheduled events.

I remember talking with a grandmother about her shift at Walmart, her hobbies, and the challenges facing her family. She didn't talk about the pay, but she was concerned about the commute—three hours round-trip for a seven-hour shift. That means she spent approximately 40 percent of her time waiting and returning, and doing it all while not on the clock.

I also met a man who was living with his mother because he had recently moved back to South Carolina from Augusta, Georgia, and was having a difficult time finding employment. He had a criminal record. His concern at the time was having to work fewer hours because of Obamacare. As he explained it, health care was in the way of working 40 hours a week, and he had been reduced to 28 hours.

This was required to meet the regulatory burdens of a forty-hour workweek as mandated by Obamacare, which would make them qualify for health benefits that his employer simply could not afford. Therefore, he was about to lose his job, or 25 percent of his pay in order for his employer to avoid having to pay the penalty or the extra expense of his presence. This was one of the unintended consequences of the health-care law for so many people, and one I had actually spoken about multiple times back in Washington. Folks were literally losing their income, or at least a significant part of it, because of the unrealistic expectations of bureaucrats trying to create government-run health care. In talking with him, I knew instantly that my fears surrounding Obamacare were true.

I learned quickly that people are more willing to be open and honest, while leaving partisan complaints aside, when they are just talking with another dude on the bus. I wasn't United States senator Tim Scott, but rather someone else using the bus to get to work. That level of honesty is hard to come by for a senator. It was incredibly helpful to have a firsthand understanding of policy implications on the people I serve.

Eventually, I let my staff at least help me choose some of the spots where I could work next. I worked in the warehouse at Goodwill in Greenville, and I swept the floors at Moe's Southwest Grill on King Street in downtown Charleston. My Opportunity Agenda was designed around the challenges I had as a youngster. But learning about the challenges facing the poorest people in my state helped me stay focused on solutions for them, and not a bureaucratic top-down legislative agenda.

While working at the Goodwill store, I worked side-by-side with a formerly incarcerated individual. He spent more than seven years in prison, and he was looking for a way to pay back his debt to society. At the time, he was making slightly more than the minimum wage, but he never complained about it. His strongest desire was to find a way to reinvest in the community that he felt like he had harmed.

I observed a lot about his professionalism, but what I saw most was once again the story of redemption. Here was a guy who knew that he had made a major mistake, and he was willing to pay with the rest of his life for that mistake. He was not going to pay behind bars, but he would pay with his life of freedom. Though the criminal justice debate had already started, it would not come before the Senate for another five years. His story is such a powerful reminder to stay focused on rehabilitation for those who are incarcerated.

Criminal justice reform on the federal level is important because more than 95 percent of all inmates in prison will go home. Said differently, only a very small percentage are serving life sentences. Unfortunately, within five years, 77 percent of folks will return to prison. Why? Because they committed another crime. Recidivism is a major problem in our federal system today. Job skills, education, and mental health treatment are three of the key areas that we must focus on to help stop this cycle. Through different reform efforts at the state level, the statistics bear out that these three are important indicators on whether a person will return to the life of crime or not.

My focus on community safety is driven by personal experiences. It's hard to forget the day when I came home from school to find that someone had broken into our house. The place was a wreck, our TV was missing, and many other things were gone. Anyone who has had their house broken into will tell you that the greatest loss was not their TV, but rather their sense of security. It can take years to overcome that feeling. My objective in the criminal justice reform debate is to focus on rehabilitation techniques that will make the community safer. In order for a returning citizen to have a positive impact on the community, they must have the skills or treatment necessary to function within that community. If they don't, they will end up right back in prison for committing another crime, in which another community member has been victimized.

The good news is we can make that positive rehabilitation happen. Working with that kind man at the Goodwill in Greenville, who only wanted to give back to the community that had accepted him back home, gave me great hope for the future.

The next place I worked was a Moe's burrito shop. I worked side-by-side with a young lady who was looking forward to serving her country just a few short months later. She was working at the restaurant until she went into the Air Force, which she was hoping to make her career. I was excited that she had a desire to serve her community. My memory was refreshed very quickly that hard work is rewarding work. As we swept the floor, it was apparent that the young woman working with me was already in the boot camp mentality. She took great pride in everything she did. I am confident that the best is yet to come for her.

One of the many observations during my undercover boss experience was the important role of a strong work ethic complemented by a really good attitude. The one thing I thoroughly enjoyed from all my experiences was the level of gratitude that many of the coworkers for the day had. Whether it was Shakira sweeping floors, the returned citizen folding clothes and checking in books, or the grandmother at the bus stop, they all shared an optimism about the future.

We have heard many times that there is dignity in all work, and this is true because all people have dignity. I have continued to visit different locations to both understand and appreciate the jobs of today as well as to learn about the people who will be our leaders of tomorrow.

I knew that what I was doing was unusual for a U.S. senator, but I certainly was not aware just how "crazy" some people thought it was until we had a reporter join me on one excursion. The resulting story in the *Washington Post* was the talk of the Hill for a few days, and I must have gotten more questions about it from other members than anything else I had done. It was truly a great experience, and we were able to take advantage of the fact that most people across the state were still learning who I was. Eventually it became harder to stay undercover, but my undercover senator days were energizing for both me and my staff. Those who had been skeptical were now fans of my efforts.

We continued to grow in both diversity and experience. I'll never forget the day I was driving to work in the middle of winter a couple of years ago. It was raining outside, and the temperature was right around freezing. As we were pulling up to the Capitol to have my car swept by Capitol Police, I looked to the right through the pouring rain, and saw this man in his wheelchair soaking wet trying to make it up a slight incline. In an instant, I realized how fortunate I was to be sitting in a warm car, and to be able to get out of the car and walk. As it turned out, that young man happened to be Shay Hawkins, one of my employees at the time.

Shay's experience is a tragedy that he has risen above. Shay was in his thirties, working in New York City, and he had grown up in a low-income community in Cleveland. He succeeded at Ohio State and Columbia University, and he became an investment banker. Shay was thriving in the aggressive New York finance world. And then tragedy struck.

Shay was walking down the streets of New York one winter afternoon. There were two gentlemen walking in front of him, when all three of them at the same time saw a wallet sitting on the sidewalk. One gentleman went to reach and pick it up, and his friend told him to just leave it there. The two men indeed left the wallet there, so Shay did the right thing—he stopped, picked it up, identified whose it was, and made contact with the woman who had lost her wallet.

It was a Friday afternoon, and he was trying to get out of town for his niece's birthday party the following day in Cleveland so as to beat a winter storm that was forecasted to come their way. The girl who lost her wallet told Shay her boyfriend was going to come get the wallet from him in downtown New York. Shay waited and waited, and finally the girl called him and told him that her boyfriend was running a little bit late. Shay, rather than leaving the wallet there for them to pick up when he returned to New York, decided to wait so she could get her wallet back before he left town for the weekend.

This delayed his departure from New York, and this ended up changing Shay's life forever. As he drove home to Ohio, he hit a patch of ice, then slid off the side of the road and into a tree. The only thing that kept him alive was the fact that his blood clotted because it was so frigid outside. He was finally discovered, rushed to the hospital, and given emergency surgery. He told me once, "After multiple doctors come in and look at you for the fifth, sixth, and seventh time with that look on their face, it's probably not going to end well for you." He remembers telling himself that he needed to prepare to die.

He lived, but he is paralyzed from the chest down. This is a man who was an All-State wrestler in Ohio, a martial artist, a good athlete, has his bachelor's degree, master's degree, and Juris Doctor. He told me one other thing about this tragedy—that he would do it all over again. At the time of his accident, there was some friction

in the family that caused some to not talk with others. His tragedy brought them together and they are a close-knit family to this
day. Because of those improved family relations, his accident had
a silver lining. Today Shay looks like he slept with a hanger in his
mouth because he smiles all day. He has a great spirit about him.
He is living proof that overcoming some of life's hardest challenges
is possible with the right attitude and an indomitable spirit.

That cold day, seeing Shay struggling to get into work was a
picture of an American life that truly struck me. It inspired me to
work harder a little longer to find ways to bring hope and opportunity into people's lives, and more important, I was able to see
the world differently. I was able to see the world through his eyes
and his experience.

Another staffer who has blessed me with his life is Patrick,
who came to our office as a part of a program run by George
Mason University to help students with disabilities find work.
Patrick, who has autism, showed up to work a shy young man. We
had very little contact at first, as is to be expected, and our main
goal was just to make sure he was comfortable coming to work.
Patrick has helped us not take for granted that everyone is going
to have the opportunity to maximize their potential; sometimes
we need to open the door for folks. Patrick is actually opening
more doors for us now, figuratively speaking.

Recently we had our annual—not every year, but kind of
annual—employee planning session. We held it in Charleston,
and as I turned the corner, I was surprised to see that Patrick had
decided to come to Charleston. His mother was kind enough to
come along as well. She did not attend any other conference or
meetings, and she was able to enjoy her day while Patrick was one
of the team. That's just who he is. One of our team members, one of
our employees, a part of our family. Patrick engaged in the conver-

sations and workflow and enjoyed himself. He has truly become part of the office, and we are so happy for that. When he came to us, his potential had not been realized, and he is still working to reach higher and farther than before. We are now learning more from Patrick than he is from us.

Another staffer who has taught us so much handles one of the most important jobs in the office. Our case work, the service we provide to constituents in need of help with a federal agency, in South Carolina is at an all-time high, and we always need more people to work on them. We take pride in having a case work approach that looks for solutions, not simply cookie-cutter letters so folks will move on and stop calling. When I was appointed to the Senate, Senator Jim DeMint had a fantastic case work manager named Deb.

Deb has a master's degree in social work, a heart for the adoption community, and loves helping people, especially her fellow South Carolinians. That's a great quality to have when you're assisting residents with everything from expediting passports to helping them get home after a natural disaster. It's not easy for Deb, though, because she's legally blind. We have special software to make it easier for Deb to "read" email. But for some typos every now and then, you would not know she deals with this as she goes about serving our office and our state.

Finally, in order for us to understand the world we have an internship program that actually compensates some of our interns for their work in my office. The goal has always been to make sure that more people have access to Washington, D.C. and the experiences as well as the relationships that are very important for future employment opportunities. I've often said that it's easier to get a job with a relationship than it is with a resume. This may not be fair, but it certainly seems to be true nationwide and frankly worldwide. So, I've encouraged young aspiring profession-als to get on someone's team even if they are there as an intern.

The program is designed to make sure that each person who comes in will play a role in the office. Interns do not simply answer the telephones, or go through the mail, or any other seem-ingly meaningless task. We help our interns and frontline people understand that actually the most important impression left on a constituent is the person who answers the telephone.

During every session, I spend some time answering the phone with the interns so that they understand that we all play an important role on the front lines. In addition, we encourage the interns to figure out what area of the office they would like to be more engaged in. We find ways for them to attend hear-ings, prepare documents, and serve in the same role as my policy or communications teams. This has led many of my interns to become employees somewhere on the Hill. From my entire senior staff in Washington, to the person at the front desk, they were all once interns somewhere on the Hill. D.C. is a very expensive place to live, and if you are without means you typically do not have the chance to be an intern. We pay some of our interns so that we get a more diverse crop of candidates, with diversity including economic, social, and demographic backgrounds.

As you can see, our team has come together quite well.

WALTER SCOTT

During my second year in the Senate, the world started changing, both inside South Carolina and outside. Michael Brown's death and the riots in Ferguson, Missouri, in late 2014 laid bare for the entire world just how strained and complicated the relationship had become between communities of color and law enforcement. As a black man, I understood the frustration and pain. As someone who had avoided focusing on race for most of my political career, it was becoming harder and harder not to speak out.

Then, in the span of three months, my life, and the lives of so many others across the Palmetto State, would face tragedy like never before. On April 4, 2015, in my hometown of North Charleston, a man named Walter Scott (no relation) was shot to death while *running away* from a police officer.

You read that right, and it was on video. What did the video show us?

A passerby happened to capture the incident, and the video showed a dramatic scene that was 180 degrees different from what the officer wrote in his police report. Walter was seen running away from the officer without a weapon. As he was running, the officer pulled his weapon and started firing at Walter multiple times. A total of eight bullets left the officer's chamber, with five striking Scott throughout his body. Next, the video shows the officer placing something that turned out to be his Taser next to the body. What the video does not show is the officer providing CPR or any other lifesaving assistance. Instead, the officer puts a dying Walter Scott in handcuffs.

The man had been shot five times, and the officer handcuffed him anyway. This was a daytime traffic stop for a nonfunctioning brake light, and it led to the murder of another African-American male. The response from our community was surprising, because it was positive. Protests were peaceful, and there were no riots, fires, or bricks thrown. Walter Scott's family's leadership was critical, and their response was key to helping our community not explode with riots and major property damage. The family resisted Al Sharpton and other "national leaders" from turning North Charleston into Ferguson 2.0.

The release of the video broke while I was at an event in St. Louis, on my way to Denver. Joe and I watched the video at least six times while we were in St. Louis, and the images of Walter Scott being shot down still haunt my memory. I had played in those neighborhoods, and I knew the community well. My heart was broken.

I decided to cancel the rest of my trip so that I could fly back to Charleston, but first I decided to visit Ferguson the next day. It was only twenty minutes from the event the previous night in St. Louis, and I wanted to use my time wisely before the afternoon flight back home. We met with the acting police chief, mayor, and a pastor of an African Methodist Episcopal (AME) church. The local congressman, Emanuel Cleaver, sent me the phone number for the pastor; I knew it would be critical to have past experience weighing in on the growing tension in North Charleston. In visiting the local AME church in Ferguson, I had a chance to talk with the pastor of the church, and I sought his wisdom. He encouraged me to take a prayerful but strong approach to the challenges. His experience, along with the willingness of Congressman Cleaver to provide insight, speaks well of how communities can come together after a crisis.

There was no denying what had happened, yet some still wanted to wish it away. We heard everything, from "Walter had grabbed for the officer's weapon" (he was running away); to "You shouldn't run from the police" (true, but running should not equal death); to "He had problems with drugs" (he was shot in the back). It was insane, and I spoke out. The video exonerated Walter Scott completely in terms of the use of deadly force. Michael Slager, the officer, was found guilty of second-degree murder and sentenced to twenty years in prison.

During the arrangements for Walter Scott's funeral, I had an opportunity to meet with the family at one of his relative's homes.

We gathered around a dining room table with plenty of food and drinks from loved ones and community friends. I was able to learn so much about Walter as the family reminisced about their lost loved one. Sitting in the home with his mother, I wanted to do something. One of my staff members, Kathy Crawford, helped with many small tasks, including the design of the program for the funeral. We all wanted to do something, and Kathy found a way to use her passion to help the family, and she even found a printer to help us get it done quickly.

When I met with Walter's family, I promised his mother we would do everything possible to make sure this sort of thing stopped happening. We introduced the Walter Scott Notification Act in the Senate, which would require the Department of Justice to study every police-related shooting across the country, as well as legislation to provide resources for body cameras across the nation.

As I write these pages, Walter's mother, Judy Scott, has passed away. She was a God-fearing woman who lost her son but prayed for peace in the community and for justice. She knew who the ultimate peacemaker is: Jesus

If a picture is worth a thousand words, then a video is worth a thousand pictures. The importance of providing law enforcement with more resources to improve the tools at their disposal is critical. A study done in Rialto, California, showed that, "after [body] cameras were introduced . . . public complaints against officers plunged 88% compared with the previous 12 months. Officers' use of force fell by 60%." This shows us that both law enforcement officers and the communities they protect are safer when body cameras are widely used.

Around the country, videos have been illuminating the challenges communities have experienced. Even when body cameras are not being used, video taken by a passerby, as in Walter Scott's case, can be of significant help. Recently in Phoenix, police threatened to shoot a family after their four-year-old daughter, unbeknownst to them, had stolen a doll from a Dollar General. Without video, we would never have known about this. We know that the vast majority of our law enforcement officers are good, honest people, but these situations happen far too often.

We can protect both officers and the public better with the use of body cameras, plain and simple. Then–Senate Judiciary Committee chairman Chuck Grassley endorsed my Walter Scott Notification Act when we introduced it, and I am still hopeful we can move it forward through the molasses that is the congressional legislative process.

On June 13, 2015, I gave a speech on the Senate floor detailing my own experiences with law enforcement. Pulled over seven times in one year. Repeatedly stopped on Capitol Hill even with my Senate members pin in clear sight. It was one of three speeches I gave that week, the other two discussing how brave the majority of law enforcement is and possible solutions for these issues, but this was the one that stuck.

Thousands of people watched on the internet and social media. Several television stations around the country wanted to talk to me. To this day, these three speeches gave me more opportunities to talk to more people than any specific event or policy that I have been a part of, and part of me is sad that it took me speaking out on one of the most persistent issues facing communities of color in every corner of our nation for that to happen. I did not earn a legislative victory, or win a fight to correct injustice; I simply told a story of what it is like, at times, to be a black man in America. And that brought what felt like every reporter in the country to my doorstep.

Why? Because I was a "successful" black man who had experienced so much of what too many African-Americans across the country experience every day? If folks ignore the fact that bias exists, then the problems will continue. We need solutions, and we need them to be well-thought-out, long-term strategies. We can never forget that we are better together.

The amazing thing is this: around this time, we started hearing stories and watching videos from police departments across the country reaching out, and communities of color were extending a hand. There were joint pizza parties where people could simply interact with officers in a nonstressful situation; officers stopped by to play basketball with kids; and an African-American pastor went on a ride-along during an officer's shift. They were showing us that while there were certainly still issues, we could begin bridging that gap with a little bit of extra effort. I wanted to help amplify that message in any way I could, and I talked with folks almost daily about the importance of bringing people together.

As I was making that case, a Nazi terrorist marched into Mother Emanuel AME, a church my uncle Joe had attended for decades. Uncle Joe had sung in the choir, served on the senior steward board, and was even awarded their "Father of the Year" award in 1997. I knew this church very well, and, on June 17, 2015, this murderer walked in and killed nine worshippers in cold blood. I am not going to use his name, as he doesn't deserve it. The killer wanted to start a race war, and he meticulously chose the oldest African-American church in the South to do so.

MOTHER EMANUEL

It's a night I will never forget. I had finished having dinner with Trey Gowdy at the Capitol Hill Club, and I was sitting in my apartment when I got news that there had been a major incident at a church. The first texts I received were from Charleston County chief deputy sheriff Mitch Lucas, informing me that there had been a shooting, it was downtown, and then that it was at Mother Emanuel. I remember thinking, Oh, my God. This is awful. As more news came in, I had the sinking feeling in my stomach that this was not only horrific, it was life altering. And it was life altering not only for me, but for Charleston. And not only for Charleston, but for South Carolina. The magnitude grew larger and larger. We were watching the news stories about Charleston, and something stirred within me. I wanted to get home immediately, but I couldn't leave until the next day.

Mother Emanuel's pastor was a state senator whom I had served with in the general assembly and a friend of mine, Clementa Pinckney. I texted him as soon as Deputy Sheriff Lucas informed me that the shooting had occurred at Clementa's church. No answer. I texted again. No answer. It haunts me to this day that my texts arrived too late. I have this text thread in my phone to this day.

As the night dragged on like the worst nightmare, and as the nation became glued to the TV, we began to learn the details of what had happened. A racist had driven ninety miles to Charleston, the place where the Civil War had started, with plans to start a race war. This young, white man walked into a black church to join a Bible study. After an hour or so, that person pulled out his weapon and in cold blood shot nine members of the church. With the accuracy of an executioner, he ended the life of nine saints. Later he would say he hesitated to go through with his plan because of how kind and welcoming they were to him. But shoot them he did.

The Reverend Clementa Pinckney. Cynthia Hurd. Tywanza Sanders. Sharonda Singleton. The Reverend DePayne Middleton-

Doctor. The Reverend Daniel Simmons. Susan Jackson. Ethel Lance. Myra Thompson. Nine names forever etched into my memory.

People outside of the state openly questioned how a premeditated act of horrific violence would play out in the birthplace of a Civil War. The murderer acted with pure motivation of stalking racial hatred, and I came home to a very volatile—and frankly potentially explosive—situation.

But this act of such hatred turned into the greatest act of forgiveness our state had ever seen. The rage was quelled not by pastors and politicians and police officers, but by the grace of nine family representatives who sat in a courtroom, staring at the killer on a television screen just thirty-six hours after he had killed the people they loved. They spoke on behalf of those who had opened their arms, pulled up a seat, and prayed with this man for over an hour, showing him so much love that for a moment—for an instant, a fraction of time—he doubted his plan to kill them all. These family members looked into the murderer's eyes, and each one said, "We forgive you."

They forgave him so quickly. They talked about how the transformational love of Jesus could impact his life. They even alluded to the fact that although their loved ones were not coming back, his life did not have to end with theirs. Matthew 5:44 says to love your enemies and pray for those who persecute you, and this one act of sacrificial love and forgiveness turned a community on the verge of eruption into an oasis of peace. It felt like the entire global community stopped and wondered aloud what in the world had happened in Charleston.

Their words stunned the entire nation, and it paralyzed us at home. Their forgiveness gripped us, holding us together like the wings of angels. The most powerful presentation of love and forgiveness injected the entire community with the antidote to what could have been, should have been, would have been one of the most explosive situations in the aftermath of a shooting.

I went to eight funerals and one wake. I felt the pain, watched as mothers and daughters, sons and fathers knew they would never see their relatives again. The pain from Emanuel lasted for months. I cried giving a speech on the Senate floor. I prayed every day for our state, for our nation, that these hate-filled terrorists would not win. I kept my texts with Clementa, including those last few that I sent and were never answered. The way his wife, and the families of all those lost that day responded, stuck with me every single day.

How could you just forgive a man like that? I was thankful, and part of me understood, but part of me was also furious that this heinous ideology had dared to rear its head in my city, my state, and at this church in particular. Mother Emanuel was started in the early 1800s, when the lives of black folks were in some ways barely lives at all. Denmark Vesey, a founder of the church, was executed in 1822 after being accused of fomenting a slave revolt. The original church was burned down by a white mob. This did not seem to be a random black church he chose, but a very specific target with very specific implications.

While we will never understand what the families of the Emanuel nine felt like, we must take pride in calling them our brothers and sisters in humanity. We may call a football catch over the middle heroic, but these everyday people, going through a horrible tragedy, are true heroes. Without them, Charleston could have been torn apart. Instead we saw massive unity walks across the iconic Arthur Ravenel Bridge, and a feeling of togetherness that I am not sure Charleston had ever felt before.

We were recovering, slowly, and continuing to try to lift the families up while trying to use this positive energy as a force to better our state. The past could not be changed, but the future could be made better. The good was reflected in the words of Daniel Simmons Jr., the son of a man killed in the shooting. As I prepared to speak on the floor of the Senate, I asked him, "Sir, is there anything you want me to say out there?"

In a hopeful voice, he said, "Yes. Remind people that we know that all things work together for the good of those who love God and are called according to his purpose."

He quoted Romans 8:28 to me. He gave me comfort, even though his father was one of those executed. My heart was overwhelmed. The very people who had the most to be angry about, those who had the most reason to be outraged, decided to allow the love of Christ to soothe their souls. They allowed the light of Christ to guide their words and their hearts in such a powerful way to extinguish this powder keg.

Politicians wanted to politicize it. The outside world wanted to detonate it. But the family wanted healing and restoration for themselves and for the community. Nothing I have ever seen before has so powerfully exuded the love of Jesus Christ, their Savior and mine. They spoke of the most powerful force on earth: not darkness, but light. The love of Jesus is that light.

MOTHER NATURE'S WRATH

Then, in October, a five-thousand-year flood hit South Carolina, devastating huge parts of the state and causing billions in damage across the Carolinas. It just rained, and rained, and rained. Sometimes it is calming to hear the rain against the window, whether you are reading a book or just trying to relax. That was not this rain.

The Weather Channel wrote, "By the time the last raindrop is counted, the October 2015 storm will go down as one of the most prolific rainfall events in the modern history of the United States." Entire towns were washed away, roads and bridges washed out, and thousands of people's homes were devastated. We had more than forty thousand households without running water, more than half of those without electricity, and entire sections of our interstates shut down.

I knew that I had a responsibility to help however I could. We went out and traveled through the water, meeting with residents and mayors to see what they needed. My staff and I were constantly on the phone with emergency officials and the Federal Emergency Management Agency (FEMA) trying to ensure resources were headed to the right places. I took a helicopter ride over parts of the flooded areas, and it honestly looked like an ocean had decided to spring up in the middle of South Carolina. I had never seen anything like that amount of water.

Mother Nature's wrath is her own, and we got an up-close and personal look. The entire year, it was as if someone had decided to test us in the hardest possible ways, all at once. But we kept moving forward. We rebuilt, came together, and stood Carolina strong. Two thousand fifteen was probably one of the hardest years in my state's history, front to back, and without the people of South Carolina there to support one another, things could have turned out quite differently. It became clear that no matter how well laid your plans, how long you take to get all your ducks in a row, there's always a bigger plan that can change everything in an instant.

The tragedies of 2015 reinforced what I had known for so many years, but I had rarely had the chance to see them on such a mass scale. We are better together when we're all pushing the car in the same direction. When we start to see certain people as enemies or scapegoats for our own problems, we end up attending funerals like Walter Scott's and those of the Emanuel nine. The cause and effect were clear as day, and heading into the 2016 elections, I felt a window of opportunity to spread our message of unity.

"It's really hard to offend someone

into changing their mind."

—Speaking to Ben Terris of the
Washington Post, May 7, 2014

CHAPTER 13

TRUMPED!

AS WE CONTINUED working to recover from these tragedies in South Carolina, a presidential election had started. If you had not already heard, the 2016 election was a groundbreaking one in American politics. And I am not talking about my Senate reelection campaign.

Half the Republicans in the country ran for president, while the Democratic race was clearly between Hillary Clinton and Bernie Sanders. As I had in 2012, I invited each Republican candidate to South Carolina for an in-person town hall with me, which we dubbed Tim's Town Halls.

As an early primary state and the first in the South, this gives South Carolina a unique place in American politics. We see presidential candidates early and often, even if it's four or eight years before they actually run. Tourists come for the beaches, and candidates come for the political buzz. (And our beaches.) Since 1980, every Republican nominee except for one (Mitt Romney in 2012) has won South Carolina. They all know this, and they all come our way.

The Palmetto State has been able to carve out this unique role because we have not only so many conservative voters, but voters that span the full range of views under the Republican Party tent. The Upstate, home to Greenville, Spartanburg, and Clemson University, is full of what you would call red-meat Republicans. It is also the heartbeat of the social conservative movement in the state, which is always a huge portion of the Republican voting bloc.

As you move down to the coast, historically you shift toward more moderate, business-focused Republicans. They are more interested in trade and regulations and offer more middle-of-the-road candidates a chance to curry favor. There has also been a significant influx of Republicans from above the Mason-Dixon Line, which aids in this shift toward a more moderate average voter from Charleston down to Hilton Head Island and the Georgia line.

With that background, in 2012, we developed Tim's Town Halls as a way to bring my constituents closer to those seeking their votes for president. So often we see highly controlled campaign events that don't always give John and Joan Smith from Beaufort the chance to actually ask the questions they want answered. Our town halls looked to change that, with a question-and-answer format and oftentimes a chance to meet the candidates face-to-face at the end of the event. We had eight town halls in 2012, including every major Republican candidate, and they were a huge success.

In 2016, we set out to do it again, which proved to be a much taller task with seventeen (*seventeen!*) Republican candidates running. We had a town hall with almost every Republican that ran, ranging from thirty people with George Pataki in Beaufort

County to more than four thousand people with Ben Carson at Bob Jones University. Donald Trump and I chatted in front of 2,500 people in Columbia, and Carly Fiorina gave her case to around four hundred people in Aiken. We ended up doing sixteen in total, with every candidate but Chris Christie. We had Governor Christie scheduled in Florence, South Carolina, but when the Republican National Committee scheduled a candidate debate on the same date, our event was canceled.

In addition to folks coming to seek votes, the town halls also showed me one of the benefits (or drawbacks, depending on who is asking) of being an elected official in South Carolina—that everyone running for national office wants your attention. The endorsement game is huge as primaries come and go, and as a statewide officeholder my phone was ringing often. In the end, these town halls served a dual purpose not just to help the people of South Carolina learn more about the candidates, but for me to talk with them a bit offstage and see where they stood on the issues most important to me.

I saw 2016 as a chance to recharge the Republican Party, and to find a generational candidate that would bring us into the twenty-first century in a lot of ways. One of those ways was shifting how we thought and talked about poverty and helping low-income families through conservative solutions, so we held a special event beyond our normal town hall series.

I cohosted an Opportunity Summit with the Jack Kemp Foundation, led by Jack Kemp's son Jimmy, and Speaker Paul Ryan in January 2016 in Columbia. We invited each candidate to come share their views on how we could help those in need across the country. Notably, Donald Trump and Ted Cruz did not come, but every other major candidate appeared. This was not an event for platitudes, but one where we were focused on getting in-depth answers on issues like education, the social safety net, and how our nation's antipoverty programs could be revamped, revitalized, and replaced with conservative solutions.

I had known Marco Rubio in the Senate for a few years, and at this event he reaffirmed to me just how much he cared about these issues. His mom was a maid, which I connected with as my grandmother was the same, and we bonded over a similar vision of the future for our nation. We knew that diversity is part of what makes this nation great, and Marco's ability to connect with both the issues that are important to me and audiences beyond the traditional Republican voter was a huge factor for me. With the South Carolina primary coming just weeks after the summit, the full-court press was on for my endorsement.

Outside of his participation in a Tim's Town Hall in Columbia in September 2015, there really was not much interaction with Donald Trump or the Trump campaign. His efforts were driven from afar through a vigorous online campaign, and he was connecting with voters in South Carolina in a way that no presidential candidate had in years. I had met Donald a few times at events throughout the years, and he was always very kind and gracious. So often you hear that his public persona is different from how he is behind closed doors with folks, and I can certainly affirm that was the case with me. But my existing relationship with Marco, and a lack of interaction and personal knowledge of Trump's vision and position on important issues, were key factors.

I eventually told Marco I was on his team, and even took his campaign team to my old house that I grew up in on Meeting Street to film a video announcing my support. I had taken Jeff Zeleny from ABC News back to the house a couple of years before, and we had walked around the outside talking about what it was like growing up there. However, this would be the first time I had been back inside that house since we left; at that point, it was boarded up and empty, but still standing. Returning to that house brought a rush of emotions, remembering hungry nights and hard days, and now I was back here filming a video announcing my endorsement for president of the United States. Only in America could someone come back to the porous house of their youth, one with holes seemingly specially tailored for mice to run in, and do so while making a presidential campaign commercial.

While we were filming the video, Marco was in Iowa, and earned a strong third-place showing. We were going to release my endorsement the next day, but a rival campaign leaked it the night of the Iowa vote in order to try to bury the news. It was one of those 3-D chess moves we hear so much about. The attempt did not work, as my phone and my campaign staff's phone were blowing up all night with reporters wanting to confirm the news. So I was now a South Carolinian going where perhaps none had gone before—New Hampshire in February.

It was cold—lung-burning cold—which was something I hadn't really experienced since we were living in Michigan. But the people were kind, and Marco was surging. Trump and Cruz were still the favorites, but Marco was right there with South Carolina still to come. Momentum was on his side for sure.

But politics is a funny game. It only takes thirty seconds to completely derail a strong campaign. That's what happened when Chris Christie decided he was going to try to end two campaigns in one night at the New Hampshire debate. It was clear immediately that Christie was looking to take Marco out, and he was able to do so through a repeated attack that made Marco's answers sound robotic. The attacks negatively impacted Marco, and it took a toll on the campaign. After a huge showing in Iowa, and while we were thrilled to bring him down to South Carolina, Rubio sank to a fifth-place showing in New Hampshire. Momentum was no longer on our side.

Marco needed a reboot, and the good news was that South Carolina was still the next stop. Trey Gowdy had also endorsed Marco, and so off we went. Flying in little planes from one part of the state to another, the adrenaline rush of going from rally to rally, I can say the feel of a presidential campaign, even when you are not the actual candidate, is hard to replicate. We would start the day on the coast, and end at a nighttime rally with the Clemson College Republicans being as loud and energetic as Death Valley on a Saturday.

At our first stop, the arena was packed like a UFC championship match, and I was going to be the announcer. My introductions were less presidential campaign and more like Michael Buffer before a boxing match. I would lower my voice, and make it as booming as possible; ladies and gentlemen, here he is, MARCO RuuuuuuuuuuuBIO! And the crowd would take that energy, make it their own, come to their feet, and start chanting "Marco, Marco!" It was a huge rush, the closest to playing in an NFL football game I had ever felt.

We shouted from the rooftops for two weeks, with Marco's poll numbers slowly but surely recovering. Lady luck was on our side, and Marco's surge started slow and steady. Governor Haley endorsed Marco the week of the primary, and we had a true Dream Team heading into election night. Marco scratched and clawed and eventually got second place in the South Carolina primary, edging out Ted Cruz. That was a great result considering where we had started, and the campaign had some momentum moving forward. However, second place still meant double digits behind Donald Trump, and it was clear what direction the Republican nomination was tilting toward. We were unable to replicate the excitement of South Carolina, and Marco's campaign stalled out fairly quickly. It would now be a race between Trump and Ted Cruz.

I decided to stay out of the remainder of the primary, reasoning that I had already endorsed and there was no need to do so again. South Carolina had passed, and the candidates had moved on to the later states in order to try to reach the number of delegates needed to secure the nomination. That did not stop the media from asking; however, I did not see the need to keep relitigating my decision. The press was relentless, from vote to vote, walking down the halls, even at lunch. My chief of staff, Jennifer, was elbowed in the face, and my press secretary almost fell down an escalator. You would think folks would want to look forward, but instead the press was trying to create division by looking back.

Candidate Trump won Iowa, New Hampshire, and South Carolina, and it became clear he was the presumptive nominee. One of the results of the 2016 primary was that the candidate with the most money raised did not win. Donald Trump, the richest candidate without question, actually spent the least amount of money throughout the primary. What he proved to us was that money raised is not the primary predictor of election outcomes. He capitalized on the social change that occurred during the Obama years, including a weak support of the military, coupled with tremendous grassroots and earned media, to accomplish a task that a few short months earlier seemed not only improbable but impossible. Candidate Trump proved to be the most interesting and provocative candidate of the past fifty years. He saw and shared the disillusionment and frustration of the average GOP primary voter, and spoke to them in ways no candidate had before. His success led to a significant amount of frustration among Democrats, who were not prepared to deal with the groundswell of support he was receiving.

There is no doubt that the rhetoric on both sides in 2016 further stained discourse in the public forum, from Hillary Clinton's "deplorables" to "lock her up." It was an evolution of a trend that began years ago. That corrosion in the public forum requires rethinking one's approach to public service. While public service remains the greatest honor in my life, it does require some heightened awareness and security at times. I remember back to my days on county council when I first started receiving death threats. In the late 1990s, after receiving a few threats, I turned them over to the Charleston County Sheriff's Department to start investigating. It was a bit unsettling at first, as it does take a little time to get used to death threats. I should say, perhaps no one actually gets used to death threats; you just learn to move on and live your life as normally as possible while making the necessary adjustments to your immediate surroundings.

The threatening letters continued for some time, and ultimately I was blessed by an aggressive law enforcement agency. Longtime sheriff Al Cannon has always been responsive to the needs of elected officials of all stripes, whether Republicans, Democrats, or nonpartisans. He takes his job and responsibilities quite seriously, and I am eternally grateful for that.

In January 2011, the very first week I was a member of the House of Representatives, Gabby Giffords was shot at a constituent event in her Arizona district. That opened a lot of eyes as to the increasing dangers of public service. She was doing exactly what we all did, going out in the district to meet with the people she served, and it ended up changing her life forever. While we may disagree on some of the solutions, I will always be in awe of her strength and passion despite the challenges she has faced.

In 2012, when I was still a member of the House, a man approached me in a local sandwich shop and was quite physically aggressive. He was very upset I refused to join the Congressional Black Caucus, among other things, and there was no doubt the situation was escalating. Attacks on other members were certainly in the back of my mind. Thankfully, along with my good friend Mikel Benton, a former law enforcement officer, I was able to defuse the situation. But it served as a stark reminder of the possible dangers awaiting.

I also used to play on the congressional baseball team for the Republicans, and despite my lack of baseball talent, I thoroughly enjoyed the competition and the camaraderie that comes from playing on a team. After deciding my energy was better spent cheering the team on, my friends and colleagues continued to show up to practice early weekday mornings, as early as 5:45 a.m., to play and raise money for charity. One friend on the team is Steve Scalise. Just two years ago, as Steve and many others practiced for the game, a deranged individual approached the field and opened fire at the players practicing.

Because Steve was in House leadership, he had law enforcement there with him; they were able to take down the assailant and stop the gunfire, but not before Steve was hit more than once. He almost lost his life, and certainly his recovery was painful both physically and emotionally. Steve is still in Congress, serving his nation that he loves and his state who loves him. I've often thought to myself what would've been had he not had a security detail. I am thankful that lives were saved because police officers stepped in and took control of the situation. Incidents like these are why I'm quite serious about my own security.

In 2017, we received phone calls so extreme that a man ended up incarcerated; the death threats were serious enough for the FBI law enforcement to get involved. We had to warn my entire staff in all four of our offices to be on the lookout, and it was a particularly intense situation. I am so thankful for law enforcement over the years, as they work every single day to keep us all safe. Our nation needs a reset on the level of toxicity and violence that we're seeing throughout our culture. We as individuals are responsible for our own actions, and we must make the decision to deescalate and refocus if we are to experience a healthier public life.

While some want to point to 2016 as a tipping point, the vitriol far predates President Trump's election in 2016. All sides must take responsibility; it is not a political problem, but rather a people problem. There is no doubt that President Trump has an aggressive style, and in the three years since his election, that has not really changed. I have been happy to work with the president on issues we agree on, such as tax reform, deregulation, and Supreme Court nominees. When I feel he has made a mistake, I will continue to speak out. As the president has continued to invite me to the White House, I have been in the Oval Office and formal dining rooms more often than I ever assumed I would, on issues from Charlottesville to trade. Thankfully, I have found that the president is willing to listen, even if he disagrees with you.

I have no idea what 2020 holds for us, but I do know that it has the potential to be a huge milestone in our nation's history. Will we find a way to come together, or simply let our divisions keep pulling us apart? Will the far-left socialist leanings of the Democratic Party come to the forefront? Socialism has been tried all over the globe, and as examples such as Venezuela show us, it never works. Despite that evidence, policy discussions in Washington have never been so difficult, as the two sides are so far apart.

We will have to wait and see what happens in 2020. But I know that no matter what happens, and regardless of what some people want you to believe, there is no overnight fix.

"Success is created in studio apartments and garages, at kitchen tables, and in classrooms across the nation, not in government conference rooms in Washington."

—FROM MY RESPONSE TO THE 2014 STATE OF THE UNION ADDRESS

CHAPTER 14

THE SCALES OF JUSTICE

WE ALL KNOW that Donald Trump's presidency has been anything but quiet. Democrats seem to be in a trance with one goal in mind—overturning the results of the 2016 election. Instead of doing their jobs working for the people of their states and districts, my colleagues on the left continue to waste time on endless investigations that have made clear they are not seeking the truth, but rather what they want to hear. The national media has only been too happy to aid in this exercise, capitalizing on division and hyperbole in exchange for clicks and viewers.

The truth is, some generational progress has been made. The president and the Republican-controlled Senate are making amazing progress: tax cuts, record low unemployment, wage growth, VA reform, judicial nominees, criminal justice reform, and many other areas.

Some of the hardest legislative battles literally take decades to win. When you introduce a bill in Congress, experts will tell you that it will take ten years of advocacy, coalition-building, and media attention for it to have a reasonable shot at becoming law.

I will be honest, the first time Jennifer told me that back when we were in the House, I was not a fan. A couple of years later, when my Senate legislative director, Charles, reaffirmed it, I still was not a fan. Remember, I had served in local politics for almost fourteen years, and I was used to getting things done quickly.

We have too many critical issues for us to waste years wandering through the wilderness, or as it is better known now, the swamp. Special interests, egos, and all sorts of unexpected factors can stall even the best efforts. Two areas where it's historically been difficult to make any progress are tax reform and criminal justice. In the past three years, we have passed important legislation dealing with both.

I addressed Opportunity Zones in depth at the beginning of the book, and they remain my proudest legislative accomplishment. They were also part of a much larger effort to overhaul our nation's tax system and put more money back in the pockets of hardworking American families.

When a presidential election is coming, every member of Congress starts to make two plans. One is what they will hope to accomplish if their own party wins the White House, and the other is if they do not. The same goes for each party as a whole in the House and Senate, and as the election gets closer and closer those priorities come into focus. With 2016 being such a wild ride, that planning period was murkier than it had ever been. Democrats were absolutely convinced that Hillary Clinton would win, as did many Republicans.

We did, however, know that if Trump won, the door would be open to tax reform. Trump is a businessman and understands the importance of a tax structure built around the idea of growth, as opposed to one whose main goal is to bring money to Washington's coffers. As I am a member of the Senate Finance Committee, which has jurisdiction over tax-related issues, this meant a huge chance to affect tax policy. The last time we overhauled our tax code was 1986, and you could say a few things had changed since then.

When Trump did win, life became a whirlwind. Republicans controlled the White House, House, and Senate, and we knew the opportunity that sat in front of us from a policy standpoint. Within a few days, I received a call from Finance Committee chairman Orrin Hatch. Senator Hatch had been in the Senate since the 1970s, had voted for the 1986 tax reform, and now was going to lead the Senate effort to draft tax reform legislation. We had fifty-one Republicans, and that very slim majority was our chance to affect generational change.

As a junior member on the committee, I was hoping to play a small role in putting the bill together. But what Senator Hatch offered that day turned into something of which dreams are made. He did not go into too much detail, but he asked me to study up on the individual portion of the tax code, keep it quiet, and, biggest of all, yes, please, keep it quiet. I knew from the tone of the conversation that it meant I had a chance to play a significant role in the process.

I spent the next few months poring over charts, graphs, spreadsheets . . . it may sound a little boring, but as I mentioned previously, I love numbers. I took a deep dive on the history of our tax system, from how John F. Kennedy authored one of the largest tax cuts in our history, to how the instability of the 1930s led to some interesting decisions being made. Luckily, my insurance and entrepreneurial background meant that I actually enjoyed all of this. Numbers are my friend, as odd as that sounds.

Early in 2017, Senator Hatch brought me together with Senators Pat Toomey of Pennsylvania and Rob Portman of Ohio and told us we would be the small team driving the process forward. The entire Senate Finance Committee would of course still work on ideas and put the bill together, but logistically it made sense to have a smaller team keeping everything on track from a foundational level.

The three of us made for an odd group, for sure. Pat is a financial services and banking wizard and had a lot of success in the financial sector before becoming an elected official. He's not one to make a show of things and is one of the most committed conservatives on the Hill. Luckily, I found out pretty quickly we had one major thing in common—we both liked to get out of Washington and back home as quickly as possible when the voting week ended.

Rob is a lawyer who has worked in multiple presidential administrations in high-ranking positions such as the U.S. trade representative and director of the Office of Management and Budget. No one knows better how the ins and outs of the federal budget work, and he is never afraid to share his opinion on things.

They had both been in Congress since the 1990s, and on the Finance Committee much longer than my two years at that point. I am forever thankful for the chairman's confidence in my abilities, which enabled me to take another step forward in accomplishing my mission of positively affecting a billion people.

As we approached the summer, we had a framework in place. We knew that we would be doubling the child tax credit and the standard deduction, adjusting the individual rate brackets, and lowering the corporate tax to engage more business growth. But having a framework is far from being done. Chairman Hatch allowed Senator John Thune from South Dakota to join Portman, Toomey, and me, and we became known as the "Core Four."

We worked tirelessly for weeks and months. We listened to other members' concerns and ideas daily. There were six o'clock meetings every night and calls long into the night. We had to continually meet with the House and White House to make sure everyone was still moving in the same direction. It was honestly the most excited I have ever been as a United States senator from a legislative standpoint.

Democrats, of course, tried to tear everything apart. Never mind that we were lowering taxes for single moms and working-class families; there were political points to be scored. I took heat for a throwaway phrase I used at a press conference, saying the whole point of tax reform was so families could "Keep Yo' Money." I was accused of being a puppet, that Mitch McConnell told me to say that so black folks would listen to us. But I have fought for lower taxes my entire political career; cutting taxes was the foundation of my campaign for Congress in 2010. Honestly, I didn't know whether that was hilarious, distressing, or just plain hypocritical. When you're sitting in the barber chair with a bunch of guys joking and ragging on each other, you are not exactly discussing the fine details of your economic portfolio as it relates to present world economic conditions. But no stone must go unturned in the fight to discredit the other side.

When it became clear that no Democrats would be willing to cross the aisle and actually work with us, our entire focus became keeping the Republican caucus together. Senator Rubio wanted a larger child tax credit and told us straight up he would not vote for the bill without one. So, we figured out how to make the math work, and Marco stayed on board. Susan Collins was concerned about the SALT deduction, so I was dispatched to find a solution that would work for her and Maine.

On and on it went, until the vote actually came. Even in the days before the vote, it was unclear whether the bill would pass. We knew we had a strong bill, and one that would help American families immensely. Through procedural shenanigans, Democrats had ensured that the individual tax cuts would sunset in the 2020s. It would have taken no more than a handful of Democrats to join us and make the tax cuts permanent, but partisan Washington again got in the way. Instead of working with us to make them permanent, Democrats tried to score political points by saying they were only temporary. That was, of course, a decision they made on their own, but heaven forbid those facts get in the way.

The week came to vote, and I was excited, anxious, and nervous all wrapped in one. We continued to make minor changes that certain members felt necessary to support the bill, and with Christmas fast approaching, I could tell a huge Christmas present was coming for the American people.

President Trump was almost out the door to head to Florida for his Christmas break when he decided to sign the bill before he left. He wanted to keep his promise of getting the tax-cut bill signed before Christmas. Only the media were present, and he ended up passing out the signing pens to reporters, He would wait until January to have a full-scale celebatory event to mark the passage of the tax-cut package which included my dream child, the Opportunity Zones.

When that day came, hundreds of people gathered on the lawn in front of the South Portico of the White House. In addition to the audience, every person who had been involved with working on the bill was present, filling up the steps behind the President's podium. The windows of the White House were still decorated, each with a Christmas wreath. Poinsettia plants brightened the grounds. It was a joyous occasion with smiles and back-slapping among all of the Congressional leaders who had made this happen.

My mind and my emotions went straight back to the meeting I had with President Trump in the Oval Office when he asked what he could do for impoverished people, and I told him about Opportunity Zones. His support had played a powerful role in what had come to pass. That was reward enough for me!

As I thought about my own background and that of my family, I realized that in this huge crowd I had been asked to stand a few feet to the President's side. On the other side was Mike Pence, and all around us were the most powerful leaders in our government. A few minutes into his remarks, Trump was speaking about Opportunity Zones and how important they were for creating a path from poverty to prosperity.

"A very special man is here who has worked very hard on this, Senator Tim Scott. Thank you, Tim," the President said, turning and shaking my hand. "Say a few words, Tim."

My first words were to thank him for his willingness to listen to my suggestion, and then I took this rare opportunity to address those who were present or may have been watching on television.

"First, I want to say that this is not about Washington. It is not about the left. It is not about the right. It's about single moms who are looking for a reason to be hopeful . . ." I said a few words about what the new law would mean in terms of doubling the child tax credit, as well as a chance for fresh opportunities. "This is a plan that speaks to every-day Americans."

My thoughts, of course, were on my mom, and all she had sacrificed to bring me to this moment. It was a thrilling moment, to be sure, and one that made me very proud to be an American.

But I did not forget the ugly tweet that tried to make me seem like the token African-American in this process. It, as much as anything, reinforced the hypocrisy of the left that black Republicans deal with every single day. I had worked hard for more than a year, building this bill from the ground up, and it was just assumed that they just wanted a black guy onstage. Did the media as a whole care? Not really. But when a Republican says something stupid, it's a weeklong story. Stupid things deserve to get called out on both sides, not just the one that fits the narrative.

But regardless, we had won. And the American people won. Opportunity Zones were now law, as well as the rest of the tax bill. We had started to tip the scales of economic justice back toward neutral, and for an encore, we decided to tackle the scales of criminal justice as well.

There are two distinct parts of what I consider the criminal justice debate. First is what you typically think of as criminal justice reform. This means ensuring that sentences properly match the crime, and things of that nature. But the second piece is perhaps the most significant role the Senate plays outside of declaring war, and that is confirming federal judges.

I am not talking about just the Supreme Court, although that is obviously a huge component of all this, but the hundreds of judgeships most of us don't even know exist. This has taken on an even more important role as previous administrations have filled these positions with more and more activist judges, some of whom think their personal opinions matter more than the founding principles of our nation.

When I first came to the Senate, Republicans were in the minority. That meant Democrats, led by Senate Majority Leader Harry Reid, were setting the agenda. Harry was infamous for, well, for a few things, but in this area in particular. In 2014, he decided to upend decades of Senate precedent and change Senate rules to ensure that most judges could pass with a simple majority vote, as opposed to the sixty votes they previously needed to pass the first set of Senate votes, known as cloture. One of the funny things about the Senate is that many rules are based on precedent, and in this particular case, in order to change the rules, you first had to break them. You would hold a vote, rule it passed with 51 votes instead of the previously required 60, and therefore the precedent was changed. While this certainly helped Democrats pass a few judges in 2012 and 2013, when Republicans won back the Senate in 2014 the shoe was on the other foot. And we would take full advantage.

Ironically enough, we had won the Senate back in 2014 in part because of another tactic of Reid's. When a new incoming class of senators started, they asked Senator Reid if he was ready to get some things done. He responded that the new members had better get comfortable doing nothing. As majority leader, he knew the best way to protect his party was to avoid tough votes, and basically do nothing. That backfired however, and his members up for election had nothing to run on, just a vague concept of keeping the Senate in Democratic hands. Because of his Do-Nothing Senate, Republicans were back in charge starting in 2014.

Mitch McConnell honored the changes Senator Reid had made to the judicial process and kept the threshold for judges at a simple majority. We certainly could have changed the rules back, and some argued that we in fact should. But the line had been crossed, and there was no going back. The rule change was expanded to Supreme Court justices. This enraged the left after Majority Leader McConnell had followed Senate tradition in 2016 and did not allow the confirmation process for an open Supreme Court seat to move forward in a presidential election year when the White House and Senate were led by opposing parties. Even though a wide variety of Democrats had espoused the same view over the years, including then-senator Joe Biden, the Merrick Garland saga proved that their short memories had come back to haunt them.

In 1992, were there a vacancy, Biden argued, Bush should "not name a nominee until after the November election is completed," and if he did, "the Senate Judiciary Committee should seriously consider not scheduling confirmation hearings on the nomination until after the political campaign season is over."

In 2007, Senator Chuck Schumer said, "For the rest of this President's term and if there is another Republican elected with the same election criteria let me say this: We should reverse the presumption of confirmation. The Supreme Court is dangerously out of balance." Schumer even suggested that because Democrats were "hoodwinked" by the confirmation testimony of Chief Justice John Roberts and Justice Samuel Alito, no more nominees should be confirmed for the balance of George W. Bush's term, even though he had eighteen months left.

After President Trump took office, it became clear just how important Leader McConnell's decision to keep Harry Reid's rule changes would be. As of February 2020, the Senate has been able to confirm a record-breaking 192 new judges to help get our judicial branch back on track. We also confirmed two new Supreme Court justices, including one of the most intense judicial fights ever over the nomination of now-justice Brett Kavanaugh. And those on the other side have only their own members and Harry Reid to thank!

Reaching those historic judicial numbers was not easy. Two nominees in particular left me unable to support them, raising the ire of some of my colleagues and those on the right. Out of the nearly two hundred judicial nominees, I have supported the president 99 percent of the time. On two occasions the nominees had histories that I found unacceptable from a racial perspective. One had college writings that troubled me, and he displayed no discernible growth since in the area of race. I decided to interview the nominee in person as a last-chance effort. I called my congressional friends who were prosecutors, including Congressman Gowdy and a few other members. With complete clarity from the people that I trusted in the room, they all suggested that I not support this nominee and that reinforced my own conviction.

The second nominee had been involved in a black voter suppression effort during a congressional campaign. I offered this nominee three separate occasions to correct the record, and unfortunately, he was unable to convince me that he was worthy of a lifetime appointment as a judge. At the request of his home state senator, I agreed to one last meeting with the nominee. This was his last chance to show me why he should be entrusted to act impartially as a federal judge. Two minutes into the meeting, he started a sentence by saying, "Now, Senator Booker . . ." I did a double take, but I let it go. A few minutes later, he called me Senator Booker *again*. Then to complete the hat trick, he did it *one more time* before I corrected him.

Now, I know there are only two black male U.S. senators, and we have both chosen to shave our heads. We also worked together, along with the Economic Innovation Group, to develop the opportunity zones legislation in its early stages. Even though Senator Booker eventually voted against the plan in 2017, I remain grateful for all the work we did together.

I view confirming judges not just in terms of quantity, but it's quality that counts. We are rebuilding trust in our judicial system. We have confirmed hundreds of competent, fair people as judges.

And I have been forced to stop two that I did not feel met that standard. There are multiple people from those districts who could have been nominated and done a fine job, but the vetting process simply broke down. I am confident moving forward that we will do a better job on these grounds and continue to confirm strong judges that will uphold the Constitution, and not their personal goals, first.

FIRST STEP ACT

While all of this furor over judges was occurring, we were also working on the first piece of criminal justice reform. The First Step Act, as the final legislation came to be known, was another once-in-a-generation opportunity to tackle a significant problem.

I first got heavily involved in criminal justice reform after the murder of Walter Scott by a North Charleston police officer. We met with multiple criminal justice advocates, police groups, and academics to draft legislation pushing for the expanded use of body cameras by police across the country.

That turned into my joining a bipartisan working group on the larger criminal justice issues, and my eventual involvement with the First Step Act. Critical in this, and somewhat surprising, was the early support of the White House behind this effort. It is no secret that President Trump is tough on those who break the law, so to see his administration get behind this effort was absolutely critical.

Basically, the First Step Act attempted to address two major issues in the federal prison and criminal justice system. First, once people have served their time, it is too difficult for them to reintegrate into society. Often, they lack either the education or skills to get employed, and the First Step Act would address these weaknesses.

As I mentioned earlier, 95 percent of federal prisoners are going to be released. Life sentences are few and far between. With that in mind, we knew we had to do something to strengthen community safety. We put incentives in place to encourage prisoners to take educational and technical courses, so that when they returned home, they were better prepared to find a job. I grew up around quite a few folks who ended up in jail, and I saw firsthand what happens when someone loses belief in their financial future. If you don't believe there is something better for you, odds are you are going to turn to whatever is easiest for you. Oftentimes that leads people to break the law. The simple question is this: will they be prepared to support themselves, or will they recidivate?

By restoring that economic hope, we help our returned citizens see that there is something better in front of them. They can take care of their family and take pride in what they are doing every day.

The second piece of the First Step Act dealt with ensuring that people were serving time commensurate with their crime. We have seen so many stories of lives being destroyed for decades over nonviolent crimes, and we knew there simply had to be a better way. To be clear, at no point were we looking to help violent offenders, murderers, rapists, or those who can honestly never do enough time for the crime they committed. But for the nineteen-year-old caught selling marijuana? We can help rehabilitate them, without taking decades of their life away and, quite honestly, saving millions of taxpayer dollars at the same time.

In the end, after much debate, and along with a strong push from President Trump and the White House, we were finally able to get this legislation moving in December 2018, and to the president's desk for his signature. It was a victory for community safety, because these formerly incarcerated individuals will now return

home better equipped to reintegrate into their families, neighborhoods, and towns. Our goal should be to help people, not punish
them forever. I truly think we accomplished that mission here,
and our communities will be safer.

So, in just three years, we had taken huge steps in tipping the
scales of justice back toward a neutral position. The importance
of tax reform, the First Step Act, and resetting our nation's judicial branch cannot be over-stated. While the unorthodox nature
of this White House leads some to either ignore that fact or forget
it, it is impossible to deny that the future of the country has been
changed for the better.

"America is the place where anything can happen. America is the place where anyone can rise. And here, on this land, on this soil, on this continent, the most incredible dreams come true."

—FROM PRESIDENT DONALD TRUMP'S
2020 STATE OF THE UNION ADDRESS

CHAPTER 15

AMERICA 2030

WHEN I STEPPED back into the Senate chamber on the evening of February 4, 2020, the air felt tense. Just a few hours before, I had delivered a speech on the Senate floor decrying the way that the impeachment trial against President Trump was being conducted. In my view, and the view of every Republican in the chamber, the whole thing had been a charade, nothing more than the Democrats' latest attempt to nullify the 2016 election. On the front page of *USA Today* that morning, I'd been quoted calling the proceedings "a hot mess," which, looking back, is a pretty mild way of putting it. In fact, the day had been so intense that during the break, I went home and ran three miles on my treadmill, trying to purge my mind of all thoughts and to calm down before the State of the Union.

As I made my way back into the chamber, though, I felt heartened that the facts were on our side. The economy was booming, unemployment was at an all-time low, and just over $67 billion was pouring into distressed communities across the nation through the Opoportunity Zones legislation. As I had put it during my speech that afternoon, those weren't Democrat facts or Republican facts; they were just facts. By every standard imaginable, President Trump's first term had been a rousing success. I had no doubt that his State of the Union address would highlight those accomplishments and also provide an optimistic look at where our country was going. After the onslaught of lies and partisan bickering we'd been forced to endure in the preceding months, I figured we could all use a little optimism.

Just after eight o'clock, Vice President Mike Pence came into the Senate chamber to greet me and some of my other colleagues, then led all one hundred of us across the Capitol Building and into the House chamber. After a few minutes of pomp and circumstance—the cabinet coming in, the Supreme Court justices taking their seats, the flash bulbs going off everywhere—we took our seats and listened to the sergeant at arms deliver his famous phrase: *Mrs. Speaker, the President of the United States!*

President Trump came into the chamber looking triumphant, as if he'd been unaware of all the lies that had been floating around him for months. As soon as he reached the podium and began to speak, I felt proud to have supported him during the worst of the impeachment trial. As expected, the speech he began to deliver was inspiring and captivating. To this day, I believe it's one of the best State of the Union addresses that a president has ever given. A few minutes into the speech, President Trump mentioned the piece of legislation I had worked for so many years to make a reality, then surprised me by mentioning me by name.

"Jobs and investments," said the president, "are pouring into nine thousand previously neglected neighborhoods thanks to Opportunity Zones, a plan spearheaded by Senator Tim Scott as part of our great Republican tax cuts."

I was so caught off guard by the sound of my name that I remained seated as the chamber erupted in applause. Then, just as I thought it was dying down, my friends Senators Richard Burr and James Langford each tapped me on the shoulder, telling me to stand so people could see me. When I did, the applause began all over again.

In the few seconds I remained standing, I thought about how far President Trump and I had come since our first meeting in the Oval Office, and all that my team and I had been able to accomplish thanks to his unwavering support. I found it amazing that in a few short years, thanks to one frank conversation in the White House and the president's unending determination to do what we both knew was right, we had found a way to lift countless Americans out of poverty and put them on the road to prosperity. All the stories I had heard about people getting their lives back on track flashed through my mind at once. I looked forward to all that President Trump and I would still be able to accomplish.

The Democrats in the chamber, on the other hand, didn't seem quite as enthused. Even when the president spoke about things that were obviously good for everyone, they remained silent and stone-faced for the cameras. On the Democrat side of the chamber, only a few brave souls broke ranks and applauded for things like falling unemployment, record-breaking stock market growth, and the elimination of our enemies abroad. I would later learn that the only Democrat to stand up during the Opportunity Zones section of the State of the Union was Kirsten Sinema of Arizona, a great public servant who knows how important it is to put aside our differences and celebrate what unites us.

Over the course of my career in politics, I've been proud to support legislation that works for Americans. It doesn't matter whether that legislation comes from a Republican or a Democrat. If it's good for the American people, I'll get behind it. I've also been proud to share in the victories of people I disagree with.

In fact, during the most fraught political fights of our time, I've often thought back to election day in 2008, when I drove with my grandfather to the Charleston County election center so he could cast his vote for a black man named Barack Hussein Obama. As we drove together to the voting place, I felt the emotion in my grandfather's voice when he said, "Timmy, I never, ever thought this was possible, to have a chance to vote for a black man to be president . . . it just ain't no way."

In the booth, where I'd been allowed to go and help because my grandfather never learned to read, I watched as his old, work-worn hand went forward to the button. I thought of all the grueling work his hands had seen, all the years they had provided food for his family through manual labor. And how he had loved us in his own way, and how he had pretended to read the newspaper as an example for my brother and me.

It was sort of a hallowed moment for me when his finger pressed that button to send a black man to sit in the White House and govern the United States of America. I stared in awe as a tear ran down my grandfather's cheek. I was forty-three years old at that time, and the only other time I had seen a tear on his face was when my grandmother died seven years earlier.

It's true that I had my disagreements with President Barack Obama, and that's putting it mildly. But that didn't mean I was not extremely proud to see a black man ascend to the highest office in the land, or that I did not feel honored to help my grandfather vote for him.

When I consider the transformation of our nation through the course of my grandfather's lifetime and reflect on the changes he has personally witnessed, I am optimistic about where America will be in 2030. We cannot keep America great by focusing on election cycles and what divides us. Instead, we must focus on the flourishing of the American sprirt. Only then can we unleash from within the resources and focus necessary for another American century—not just for our generation, but for future generations as well.

AMERICA 2030 PLAN

Those of us who spend time as lawmakers in Washington must remember that we are designing a country for the generation that follows us. That's been part of the secret sauce of America for a long time: the generations that have gone before us have been willing to make sacrifices on behalf of future generations. They were not thinking only of themselves and their families, but of you—and your family. The folks who saved the world from the horrors of Hitler– they were literally willing to die for generations of Americans they would never meet.

I will not be in Washington in 2030, but the decisions I make today, the legislation I sponsor and vote on, are paving the path for those who will make the laws in a decade. We must remember that we are not designing a country for the next election cycle, but for the next generation. There are problems that are preventable and curable with a little courage and a little less self-interest. After all, as elected officials, we are elected to serve not ourselves, but our districts, our states, and our nation.

With the same tenacity and hope for our future that our ancestors displayed, we can design a policy structure and focus on the pillars that produce the most successful generation of Americans this world has ever known. That is why, with the passage of Opportunity Zones, I am shifting my Opportunity Agenda to a bigger focus—the America 2030 plan. To me, as a legislator, there are two major areas to work on: our education system, and workforce development for the gig economy. These are the cornerstones of my opportunity agenda.

EDUCATION REFORM

Our education system is mediocre at best. The United States is a member country of the OECD, or Organisation for Economic Cooperation and Development. All member countries have democratic forms of government, and they all have highly developed economies. But when you compare our performance in the subjects of English, math, and science, we rank in the bottom half of all OECD countries. We rank poorly against our competitors. We must improve the educational output of this country if we are going to be successful on a global scale.

The powerful foundation of America 2030 is education. In too many places in this country, too many of our kids lack the high-quality education that equips them to be competitive globally. If you cannot compete globally, then you certainly will not compete in your own communities, because our communities today are connected to a global market. For those communities to be competitive tomorrow, kids need to have a quality education today. That is missing in most of our socioeconomically distressed communities.

My good friend Trey Gowdy says that education is the closest thing to magic in America. I think he's right. You can look at our incarceration rates, unemployment rates, high school dropout rates, our lifetime average incomes—they all point back to one specific area: lack of educational achievement. For a kid growing up in 2020, in conditions similar to mine as a child, helping them get to 2021 is important. But we must think bigger. Helping them get to 2021 *on a path that leads them to success in 2030* is critical—not just for their future, but for our country as a whole. This will require us to have some uncomfortable conversations, especially regarding our education system in underserved communities.

Currently, we spend $20+ billion on Title I schools. Title I schools are the poorest schools in America, and they consistently have the lowest performances. Their poor performance is not tied to race; it is not about ethnicity; it is not merely about location. If there were a dictionary that identified the terms of our educational system, then the synonym for poor academic performance would be one word: poverty. Where the poverty index is high, the performances are consistently lower. That is true in rural America, as well as the inner cities.

While there are a variety of proposed solutions out there, such as school choice, increasing or changing funding mechanisms, and targeting resources directly to Title I, or lower-income, schools, we have not been able to find the magic elixir for decades now.

Some of the problems lie in systematic failures. We have seen our share of that in my home state; as the *Post and Courier* reported, "In November 2014, the state's highest court ruled the state fails to provide poor, rural children even the minimal education opportunities the constitution requires." Nationally, in 2018 NBC *News* wrote, "Residential segregation causes a disparity in educational opportunity because it creates higher-income communities, with predominantly white school districts that have more local tax revenue for their schools, compared to fewer dollars and resources for school districts in low-income, minority neighborhoods."

The results of those disparities are sharp. The same NBC report noted, "Schools with a majority of Black and Latino high school students have less access to high-rigor courses than predominantly white schools. For instance, the authors said, 33 percent of high schools with high black and Latino enrollment offer calculus, compared with 56 percent of high schools with low black and Latino student populations."

Clearly, our education system simply is not working for too many of our low-income children. Public education is a wonderful thing, but it must be held accountable when it fails. For elected officials, however, that proves easier said than done. Of course, it is easier to just throw money at the problem, and then to earn favor when you tell your constituents you did so. But what if the answer is rebuilding the system instead? School choice offers an avenue that provides much-needed competition, but teachers' unions and funding purists have blocked those chances for students in all different parts of the country. They are looking at next year, ensuring they keep their positions and their power, instead of considering where our students are going to be in five years. It is no shock to anyone that our poorer, minority communities on average perform worse in school.

In some cities, we are seeing high-income, formerly unincorporated areas begin to try to carve out their own new school districts to keep their children out of the city's other schools. This is one more easy way out, and while I cannot say I begrudge parents who are looking out for their children, it shows how much work we have do to as an American family. Remember, I'm the guy who almost failed out of high school. To me, the answer is very clear: give parents a chance to find the best school for their children, and they will. Period.

Every child in every zip code must have quality education choices and outcomes in order for us to live up to the highest potential this nation has to offer. I believe that we will be able to help the students in Title I schools, and distressed and lower-income communities to get a better education, and we can start doing this in a few important ways.

First, we need to create an incredibly competitive education system in America. That may require charter schools, virtual schools, and—I suspect this is true—competition in our education system. This could come in the form of magnet schools and charter schools that are all in the public arena; or it could be in private schools and parochial schools that have produced some of the greatest success stories this nation has ever seen. There are models around this country where they are already working. One classic example is the Success Academy Charter School system, in New York City. This charter school produces some of the best test scores of minority students in the country. Those test scores can be many points higher on a 100-point exam than the scores of kids living in inner city metropolitan areas and other distressed parts of the country.

In America 2030, I want to see more people aligning themselves with the country's best interests at heart. I do believe that this interest is best met and served through a conservative construct. That's what happened all over this nation—sixty, eighty, one hundred years ago. It's one of the reasons why many of the best colleges and universities in the world are in America: it's because our ancestors had invested so much for so long in a K-12 system that produced excellent students. There was enough talent to go around, and this created fertile ground to create strong colleges.

Today, we still have the best colleges and universities in the world. We are also now attracting and recruiting the world's best talent. Students from China, Africa, Asia, and Europe descend upon America's higher education system to become the best-educated, the most talented, the most competitive students in the world. Then they often go back to work for companies in their countries and compete with us. We have to make sure we don't miss any opportunities for our nation to produce highly qualified, competent students, even in the poorest zip codes.

We must embrace the concept that lays the foundation for economic freedom, which is a free market system based on economic opportunity. If we can find a way to protect the marketplace as we know it, and to expand the reach of that marketplace—into corridors and neighborhoods where the dream of economic freedom is elusive or dead—then we will see a Lazarus effect in the poorest communities in our country. All of this is preceded by a strong and powerful education system in every zip code in this nation.

This brings me to the second pillar of my America 2030 plan: we must solve the needs of the future workforce. We need people to come together and find solutions that benefit as many of us as possible. It can certainly be hard to convince people from across racial, ethnic and economic boundaries that others have their best interests in mind, but that is the beauty of what made America great in the first place. If we don't have a world-class workforce in 2030, our economy is going to fall behind without a doubt.

It's one of the reasons why I've placed an emphasis on improving not only our education system, but also our workforce development programs, as well as attracting more opportunities into those communities, using my Opportunity Zone legislation.

JOBS AND OPPORTUNITIES

When my granddaddy worked for a living, he spent most of his life working for one company, and he worked for them for decades. I, on the other hand, have worked for three or four different companies so far. The next generation will work for eleven to fifteen different employers in their lifetime. What has changed?

We live in a gig economy, a job market that is characterized by the prevalence of flexible, temporary, short-term contracts or freelance work, as opposed to permanent jobs. Our work economy is powered by technology, which means location is not an issue; many people can work from anywhere in the nation. Unlike my granddaddy, we are not destined to live in the same city where our jobs are located. I have dozens of friends who work from home because they would rather live somewhere else than where their company or job is located, and this has created amazing opportunities for people all around this nation—and frankly, around the world. We should be pretty excited about the prospects and possibilities of a better future in the gig economy. Under President Trump, we are at a 50-year low rate of unemployment. We have more jobs open than people looking for work. Essentially, if you want a job, you can find one. However, if we don't focus on workforce development, apprenticeship programs, and job training, we may eventually have more jobs than we have people. The people we will have will be unable to fill some of the open jobs, because of their lack of skills or specific training. Not only do we need to be aware of the transformation that's happening in the post-industrial America, we must also be keenly aware of the important training for a lot of folks who may be displaced by this gig economy.

The technology will give us real flexibility, a more resilient economy, and one that is not driven by simple business prospects. It will be driven by well-trained candidates who will make America's economy the shining star in the global business.

Change starts with K–12 education, and it moves into workforce training and technical colleges. We can ensure that college is more affordable for kids who earned the right to choose a school of their choice, but who could not afford to attend it. We must be united in our efforts to move forward, and make sure that every American has opportunity knocking on their front door.

There is also a significant part of achieving these goals that has nothing to do with government at all. On the ground level, from our neighborhoods and communities on up, we must have the motivation to do these things on our own, instead of depending on others to make it happen.

INVESTMENT

We have 50 million Americans living in distressed communities, and more that $2 trillion of unrealized capital gains, just sitting there. We should incentivize those dollars to be invested in those communities. My vision for America 2030 seeks to create a path for private sector dollars to be invested in distressed communities.

Getting friends who are diametrically opposed onto the same page is a difficult task, but we succeeded in that difficult task as we worked on Opportunity Zones. President Trump signed legislation that promoted, encouraged, and frankly inspired a nation to take a second look at legislation that had no chance of succeeding without his approval. In the incubator of legislative creativity was Cory Booker and my staff, working together to come up with certain policy positions that we felt would be successful in a broader political landscape.

Cory and I have very little in common from a policy position. But instead of focusing on the things we did not have in common, we were able to partner together and work for over three years on the Opportunity Zones legislation, which was a collaborative effort between his office and mine. Unfortunately, in the end, Cory did not vote for the president's tax bill that included the Opportunity Zones legislation.

More good news due to the policies of the Trump administration: For the first time in a long time, our overall poverty rate is down to about 12.5 percent, from a 15 percent high just a few years ago. It has been stubborn since the early 1970s, when the poverty rate was around 14.5–15 percent. The difference is about 8 or 9 million fewer people living in poverty—these are real people who now have hope! That was the result of President Trump's policy positions whereby he has reduced taxes and reset regulations to a far more responsible, not oppressive, level.

For this country to function at the highest level, members of Congress need to work in a bipartisan fashion. If we can find areas of agreement, even when we disagree on 95 percent of the topics, when we find that 5 percent, if we've developed enough rapport and credibility across the aisle, we will do the most astonishing things.

The benefits will go to the kindergartner in 2018 who has the good fortune of graduating in 2030 in a country whose leaders are working together for their wellbeing and success, the success of the graduating student in 2030. Not our own as elected officials.

AMERICAN EXCEPTIONALISM

The concept of American exceptionalism is when people do things for others, not because there is a reward or benefit for themselves. American exceptionalism is driven by the concept of putting someone above yourself, and we as a nation are exceptional because of God, our freedom, and our democracy. American exceptionalism is a higher calling to a greater purpose.

Back when I was on county council, I witnessed firsthand the power of a community displaying their exceptionalism. In 2007, a Stratford High School student named Brittany Riffe was on her way to a student government meeting in Goose Creek, a suburb of Charleston. Brittany and a few of her friends were driving down

St. James Avenue, and suddenly, the car hit the side of the curb. The car flipped over three and a half times, and because Brittany was lying in the backseat, she was partially ejected from the car. As the car came the rest, she had broken her back in two different places. Brittany was paralyzed from the waist down.

This tragic accident happened two days before the start of her senior year. The situation reminded me of my own car accident when I was her age, when I flipped my car a few weeks before the start of my senior year. I remember being so devastated by the loss of my football season, but Brittany's injuries were so much worse. My accident happened in 1982, and Brittany's was in 2005—almost twenty-five years later, to the day. I sat in my favorite restaurant, California Dreaming, as I read the story of Brittany's car accident, her courage, and her strength. I knew I had to do something.

I learned what hospital she was in, and I went to her room to tell her how she had inspired me. Now, I don't advise just showing up at someone's hospital room. When the family sees a face they don't know, it can be startling. Fortunately, they recognized me because I was the chairman of county council at the time, but still they cautiously and carefully wanted to discern why I was there. I don't blame them.

After a few rightfully inquisitive moments, we landed in a good place. They understood I was there with good intentions in my heart. I shared my experience with my car accident back in 1982, and I told them how impressed I had been with Brittany's attitude. I wanted to do something for her that would help restore her confidence and strengthen her hope even more.

So many times in my life, people have stepped up and provided Christmas gifts, food, and even clothing when we could not afford it as a family. Sometimes the help came from a family member, and other times it was people in the community who simply wanted to help. When I found out that Brittany's eighteenth birthday was just around the corner, that was all I needed to know. I organized an eighteenth birthday party with some help from friends throughout the community.

Everyone I called was willing to chip in. George Fennell would provide the hotel space for a party. Eddie Stokes of Stokes Honda agreed to pay for half of a new vehicle, as Brittany's family could not afford the handicap-accessible vehicle she would need moving forward. My good friend and mentor Al Jenkins owned a beautiful antique car, and he was willing to auction it off and donate the proceeds as resources for Brittany's vehicle.

As a team, we got to provide Brittany with a new handicap-accessible vehicle, as well as thousands of dollars in cash. I walked away from that experience feeling blessed beyond words. I felt blessed by a young lady with an indomitable spirit, blessed by a community that responded to a terrible tragedy simply by being asked, and blessed by faith that called me to action. Romans 8:28 reminds us that all things work together for good.

Time and time again, whenever I am concerned about where America is going and how we maintain the glue of our nation, I'm reminded of stories like Brittany's. So often, good people can come together to help someone in need. They invest in others, simply because they can. Not because there's a program, and not because there's a tax deduction. Simply because they can.

BETTER TOGETHER

We are absolutely better together. The sooner we realize that, the better off we will be. Brittany's story is just one example of a community coming together, regardless of the color of our skin, no matter the resources in our pocket, and unimpeded by any obstacles in our way. We just know that it is our responsibility to help. In Brittany's story and many others, people continue to invest in others, with no question about return.

I've reconnected with Brittany, and she's doing really well. She graduated from my alma mater Charleston Southern University. She has a little boy, and she is involved in our church. Life has not been easy or simple for her, but she is not a victim—she is a victor! I am very confident that her best years are ahead of her, and the joyful miracle of her life shines brightly into mine.

I have no doubt we can achieve all of the greatness that still lies in front of us. I have seen the worst of America, and I have lived the best of America. Nowhere else on the planet is that possible, not on the scale it is here. No matter where you are from, no matter your family history or your zip code, America 2030 offers every American the opportunity to succeed.

Opportunities are the answer to success. We live in a country built on the foundation that all men are created equal. We are endowed by our Creator with certain unalienable rights, including life, liberty, and the pursuit of happiness. That is not just the principle; it's a foundational concept. Our notion of American exceptionalism is not based on any individual or race, but on the premise that each of us has the right to pursue our highest potential. Unlike almost any other country on earth, we aspire to a definition of equality and fairness that allows for anyone from anywhere at any time to rise to the highest levels of success in this nation. This country consistently and continuously reflects progress, and if we embrace what's possible, we will live a future we thought impossible.

America 2030 is a dream and a plan for what is possible in this nation when we have people helping people. It is not a focus on the leaders in Washington, because we should not assume that the 535 decision makers in Washington have a better perspective on how to improve communities than those who are actually living in the communities. That is a false aberration, and it is not real. Our strength is in our people. When we simplify and shrink the impact Washington has on your daily life, we are also telling communities to keep their money, equipping you to make your decisions, instead of making your decisions for you. When healthier communities are woven together, they create healthier states and a healthier nation.

When people do things for others, not because there is a reward or benefit for themselves, then America becomes truly exceptional. Think of those kindergartners and their unlimited dreams. Consider the kind of future we should create for them. The opportunity is knocking; we just have to answer the door.

ACKNOWLEDGMENTS

THANK YOU to Ben Ben, aka the heir to the Scott throne! You have motivated me and strengthened me to keep raising the bar. You remind me often that leadership is caught not taught. May we continue to find our time mutually beneficial!

To Ben, my brother and faithful friend! You absorbed much of the pain during our childhood and still became the strongest person I know. Your selflessness in serving our country has been and continues to be the model for future generations. You and Drina bless me with powerful leadership.

To Mia, your journey and tenacity strengthens our family everyday. Thank you for the blessing of Ben III.

Nita, thank you for all the Christmas miracles that meant so much to us as kids. I could not have been blessed by better people than you, Clyde and Kendra.

There are too many family and friends to name individually but let's try anyway: To Otis, Brandt, Stringer, Joe McKeown, Al Jenkins, the Brian Moniz, and family, JDC, MEB, Roger Young, Mikel, Jack Goude, Brian Goff MJS, Kevin McCarthy, and Trey.

Without my grandparents, mom and brother there would be no stories to tell.

Without incredible mentors like John Moniz, Al Jenkins, Ed Bryant, and so many others I would have never found my path. Thank you all.

Without the consistent dedication and hard work as well as the watchful eyes of Roger, Joe, Tricia, Kate, Sean, Henry, Jennifer, and Cynthia, this book would not be complete!

Without faith none of it is possible. I'm thankful to all my pastors especially, Greg Surratt who has provided faithful instruction and directions for the last twenty years. To the late A.R. Blake, former pastor of Morris Street Baptist Church, the gift of scripture grows stronger every day because you planted the seeds early in my life. I'm grateful also to Reverend Joy. May the blessings of Luke 6:38 grow ever stronger in the minds and hearts of readers who take the challenge of living what they believe and not simply what they see.